NASTY

SOPHIA
AMORUSO

—

Foreword by
Courtney Love

GALAXY

NASTY GALAXY

FOR MY PARENTS, MY HUSBAND,
AND OUR POODLES.

FOR THE TEAM, OUR CUSTOMERS,
AND THE GIRL WHO DOESN'T YET
KNOW SHE'S A GIRLBOSS.

FOREWORD / Courtney Love

I first heard of Sophia years ago through my daughter. Sometime in 2015 we were introduced by a mutual friend who thought we might get along, both personally and professionally, and could potentially do something together. He was right. We worked on a collaboration called Love, Courtney that launched just in time for Valentine's Day 2016.

I was immediately impressed by Sophia: by the fact that she is cool and has great taste, but also that she is so professional. My first thoughts: Wow, is she controlling, but I totally get it—that's how you get things done. The people who come out on top pay attention to their business. At one point, I was an exotic dancer, but for every $5 I made on the stage, I put $3.50 toward my band, and never deviated from that formula. This is how you build something great and Sophia gets that.

I know thirty girls who had the same origin story—a vintage store on eBay. It's not an original idea. But Sophia named hers after a funk singer's album and knew the rest wasn't about being lucky—she played the system and she played it hard. She didn't get any big breaks, she didn't know anyone special, she isn't the daughter of someone connected or famous. But she *is* cool, she has been talking to her customers from the beginning, and she's incredibly buttoned-up. There's nothing sloppy about her—she reminded me to collect nondisclosure agreements at every turn of our collaboration, she put together a media plan, and she positioned it perfectly. Because Sophia doesn't sit back or take chances that it will work out—she ensures that it will work out.

It's hard for me to give this advice, but it's advice I wish I had been given when I was younger. Patti Smith recounts that Williams S. Burroughs taught her this when she was young: "Build a good name. Keep your name clean. Don't make compromises. Don't worry about making a bunch of money or being successful. Be concerned with doing good work. And make the right choices and protect your work. And if you can build a good name, eventually that name will be its own currency." I've learned the hard way that credibility is worth it—and I think that's something Sophia inherently understands. She's not nearly there yet—she's still on her way—but she has a strong vision, and she runs a tight ship. Now that I've gotten a chance to see how she works, I have no doubt she'll get there.

I'm a little too old to wear Nasty Gal most of the time, but my daughter loves the brand. It's really difficult to build something that is both cool and big and that resonates with a lot of different girls. As it grows, Nasty Gal will bump into things that are controversial—it might stumble at times and be criticized for getting big—but because it's a brand that has integrity, it will always be okay. And at the end of the day, you can't argue with success.

a shot from our "love, courtney" collab.

So here's my advice for all you Nasty Gals and Girlbosses:

1. Be prudent with your money. You should be spending your money and your energy on your endeavor. Have a vision that plays out into a five-year and ten-year plan. Know where you want to be in ten years. Take input from other people, especially your customers or fan base, but stay true to the vision inside.

2. If you position yourself in the failure/success model, you're going to fail. Your thinking needs to be more original and creative than that. It's victory or else. There is no other choice. All successful people have this in common. They don't even allow themselves to envision failing.

3. Adapt! Let yourself be surprised.

4. Be an early adopter, because it's fun to be the first one there.

5. Keep your nose clean.

Love,
Courtney

"She played the system and she played it hard."

@sophiaamoruso

INTRODUCTION / Sophia Amoruso

"Nasty Galaxy represents infinite possibility—a place in time and space where anything can happen."

Nasty Galaxy. It's a phrase that's been kicking around in my head for many years now. Seems almost prescient—like an elegant way to expound upon the brand I started in 2006. Ten years ago, it was just an eBay store inspired by the name of a Betty Davis album—and I've watched, in complete awe, as it's become an operating system and hub for a generation of Girlbosses. Not something I could have dreamed up in the dingy bedroom where I started it all with a laptop, a digital camera, and a pile of hard-won and haggled-over vintage clothing (see page 31). I pretty much exclusively wore eau de Febreze until 2010. Let that be a lesson: Your life can begin as a dirty skateboard and morph into a hot rod somewhere along the way. You just have to keep the doors on the motherfucker, even if it takes a lot of duct tape. It never ends: I am duct-taping all day, every day, to this day. Doesn't end. So Nasty Galaxy. What could it be? A new solar system filled with the magical spirit dust of David Bowie? Nasty Gal as a world, with all of its requisite trappings, in the most physical sense of the word?

The process of putting this book together was really difficult—until it wasn't at all. At first, I thought it could be some sort of style and lifestyle guide, even though I've always (and publically) vowed I'd never put something like that out into the world. . . . But there you go— I have the early outlines to prove that I was actually going to teach you how to mix prints. Then it morphed into a straight-up brand book—a visual counterpart to the history of Nasty Gal, until it became very apparent that the only people who would be interested in thumbing through something like that are our art directors. And then I decided to go all the way back to the beginning—to the black hole moment of creation—to trace the influences of both myself, of Nasty Gal, and of #Girlboss, and to serve it all up in stream-of-consciousness realness, not unlike your Instagram feed. It is a deep dive into my brain and my home.

Like all things that seem effortless and seamless in retrospect, I think this book makes a lot of sense now, as challenging as the path to order was to find. *Of course* this is the book. Or at least the opening play. Because here's the thing: Nasty Gal isn't just a clothing brand, and Girlboss isn't just a meme that represents women stepping into and owning their power. Just like in the Nasty Galaxy, there's no defining line or event horizon. And no moment when you have to be *just one thing.* Nasty Galaxy represents infinite possibility—a place in time and space where anything can happen. The women and artists in this book represent that—people who play without rules, who define new genres that only seem obvious in retrospect, who think in an original and boundless way, who don't even consider that "no" might be an answer. The path to join them takes guts, grit, and the willingness to step into an abyss of unknowns, with no clear path in sight. You can only see the road you've paved in the rearview window, but no matter, because there's plenty of magic ahead. Welcome to the Nasty Galaxy.

what a dreamy album. tom rapp has the most endearing lisp. too.

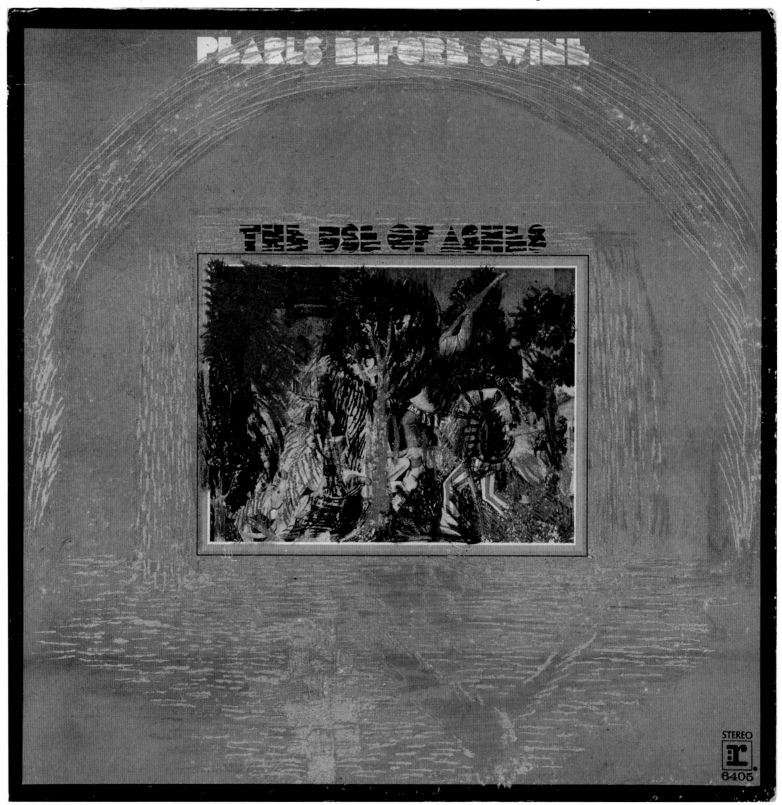

Chapter 1

PEARLS BEFORE SWINE

—

THE USE OF ASHES

"ROCKET MAN" // MY FATHER WAS A ROCKET MAN — HE OFTEN WENT TO JUPITER OR MERCURY, TO VENUS OR TO MARS — MY MOTHER AND I WOULD WATCH THE SKY — AND WONDER IF A FALLING STAR WAS A SHIP BECOMING

ASHES WITH A ROCKET MAN INSIDE — MY MOTHER AND I — NEVER WENT OUT — UNLESS THE SKY WAS CLOUDY OR THE SUN WAS BLOTTED OUT — OR TO ESCAPE THE PAIN — WE ONLY WENT OUT WHEN IT RAINED

ON SEREN-DIPITY

winter 2016.

Unless you're a YouTube star, life-changing things don't happen to you inside your house. Friends may be met on the Internet, but they are made and kept IRL. Life is meant to be lived—not in your kitchen, or lying in bed dropping your phone on your face, but with psychic juju flying around the room and all the stars aligning all up in your pretty face.

Action is the breeding ground of serendipity. What I mean to say is this: Even serendipity requires an invitation. Sure, it's cute to be a wallflower—but as they say, hope is not a strategy. Assume everything happens for a reason even if it doesn't. Do all that you can with all that you have and you'll find yourself with more than you could ever dream of. Connect dots that most wouldn't and the heavens will open up to swallow you whole. Take no moment, no person, and no single thing for granted, and you'll dance yourself into living the dream.

"Do all that you can with all that you have and you'll find yourself with more than you could ever dream of."

SOPHIA AMORUSO

19

Women who
seek to be equal
with men
lack ambition.
/
Timothy Leary

gino, our baby boy.

WELCOME TO OUR HOME. IT'S LIKE
A SITCOM IN HERE. A REVOLVING
DOOR OF FRIENDS AND FAMILY—NOT
TO MENTION PILES UPON PILES OF
WORK. THERE'S NOTHING MORE
COMFORTING THAN THREE SMALL
POODLES JUMPING ON MY LOWER LEG
EVERY TIME I RETURN. THIS PLACE
IS WHERE I FIND MY PEACE.

THE ONLY WAY TO BE PURE IS TO STAY BY YOURSELF
TOTAL SUBMISSION CAN BE A FORM OF FREEDOM
OFTEN YOU SHOULD ACT LIKE YOU ARE SEXLESS
THE MORE YOU KNOW THE BETTER OFF YOU ARE
SYMBOLS ARE MORE MEANINGFUL THAN THINGS THEMSELVES
DESCRIPTION IS MORE VALUABLE THAN METAPHOR
IT'S BETTER TO STUDY THE FACT THAN TO ANALYZE IT S HISTORY
EATING TOO MUCH IS CRIMINAL
YOU SHOULD ENJOY YOURSELF BECAUSE YOU CAN'T CHANGE ANYTHING ANYWAY
THERE'S A FINE LINE BETWEEN INFORMATION AND PROPAGANDA
CHASING THE NEW IS DANGEROUS
YOU CAN'T EXPECT PEOPLE TO BE SOMETHING THEY'RE NOT
SOMETIMES ALL YOU CAN DO IS LOOK THE OTHER WAY
ANYTHING IS A LEGITIMATE AREA OF INVESTIGATION
HABITUAL CONTEMPT OR DISGUST DOESN'T REFLECT A FINER SENSIBILITY
YOU CAN PULL YOURSELF OUT OF ANY HOLE IF YOU ARE DETERMINED ENOUGH
IMPOSING ORDER IS MAN'S VOCATION; CHAOS IS A VERSION OF HELL
HIDING YOUR MOTIVES IS DESPICABLE
TRADING A LIFE FOR A LIFE IS FAIR ENOUGH
SACRIFICING YOURSELF FOR A BAD CAUSE IS NOT A MORAL ACT
REDISTRIBUTING WEALTH IS MANDATORY
CHANGE IS VALUABLE BECAUSE IT GIVES THE OPPRESSED A CHANCE TO BE TYRANTS
IT IS HEROIC TO TRY TO STOP TIME
YOU GET THE FACE YOU DESERVE
THINKING TOO MUCH CAN ONLY CAUSE TROUBLE
YOU ARE RESPONSIBLE FOR CONSTITUTING THE MEANING OF THINGS
YOU ARE COMPLETELY GUILELESS IN YOUR DREAMS
CHILDREN ARE THE HOPE OF THE FUTURE
PEOPLE ARE BORING UNLESS THEY'RE EXTREMISTS
YOU DON'T KNOW WHAT'S WHAT UNTIL YOU SUPPORT YOURSELF
YOU MUST DISAGREE WITH AUTHORITY FIGURES
VIOLENCE IS PERMISSABLE, EVEN DESIRABLE OCCASSIONALLY
IN SOME INSTANCES IT'S BETTER TO DIE THAN TO CONTINUE
YOU HAVE NO MORE RESPONSIBILITY TO YOUR FAMILY THAN TO OTHER PEOPLE
YOU SHOULD RAISE BOYS AND GIRLS IN THE SAME WAY
AT TIMES INACTIVITY IS PREFERABLE TO MINDLESS FUNCTIONING
IT'S GOOD TO TRY TO STAY CLEAN ON ALL LEVELS
IT'S CRUCIAL TO HAVE AN ACTIVE FANTASY LIFE
THE MOST PROFOUND THINGS ARE INEXPRESSIBLE
SELF-AWARENESS CAN BE CRIPPLING
ABSTRACTION IS A TYPE OF DECADENCE
BEING BORED CAN MAKE YOU DO CRAZY THINGS
DRAMA OFTEN OBSCURES THE REAL ISSUES
CRIMES AGAINST PROPERTY ARE RELATIVELY UNIMPORTANT
DYING SHOULD BE AS EASY AS FALLING OFF A LOG
THE WORLD OPERATES ACCORDING TO DISCOVERABLE LAWS
THERE'S NOTHING REDEEMING IN TOIL
EXPIRING FOR LOVE IS BEAUTIFUL BUT STUPID
FATHERS OFTEN USE TOO MUCH FORCE
IF YOU'RE NOT POLITICAL, YOUR PERSONAL LIFE SHOULD BE EXEMPLARY
SLIPPING INTO MADNESS IS VALUABLE FOR THE SAKE OF COMPARISON
LEARN TO TRUST YOUR OWN EYES
TEASING PEOPLE SEXUALLY CAN HAVE UGLY CONSEQUENCES
THERE'S NO SENSE BEING ANYWHERE BUT THE TOP OF THE HEAP
YOUR ACTIONS ARE POINTLESS IF NO ONE NOTICES THEM
A STRONG SENSE OF DUTY CAN IMPRISON YOU
REPETITION IS THE BEST WAY TO LEARN THINGS

Jenny Holzer's "Truisms"
on display in our hallway.

1970s hand - embellished leather jacket.

Not what we have but what we enjoy constitutes our abundance.

/

Epicurus

TURA SATANA

One of those women who lived nine lives before she turned thirty, Tura Satana declined a marriage proposal from Elvis, spent time as a burlesque dancer, survived two years in a Japanese internment camp with her father, and was in an arranged marriage when she was only thirteen. Starring in movies like *Faster, Pussycat! Kill! Kill!*, she was enigmatic, magnetic, and cool. And really, really tall.

Bad Bitch of CINEMA —

I took a lot of my anger that had been stored inside of me for many years and let it loose. I helped to create the persona of Varla, and helped to make her someone that many women would love to be like. /

Tura Satana

SOPHIA AMORUSO

29

HOW TO SHUCK AN OYSTER

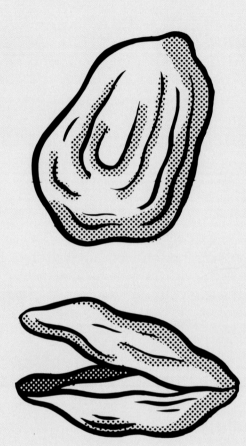

1. To start, wash your goddamn oyster.
2. Put on a big, thick gardening glove.
3. Take a knife (or buy a professional shucker, you sucker) and insert it in at a 45-degree angle where the oyster hinges are closed.
4. Worm the knife in until it's lodged between the top and bottom shells and wiggle-dee-wiggle until the thing pops open.
5. Cut the muscle that attaches the oyster to the shell, and look out for OYSTER CRABS! I found one living under my oyster once and it was disgusting.

TIPS FOR THRIFTING

31

1. Touch every piece of clothing in the store, avoiding the used-blanket section.
2. When you amass too much to carry, start a pile and guard it with your life.
3. Check for stains, smells, and dusty rotten linings—if it's too fucked up, skip it.
4. Around Halloween is a great time of year to shop—thrift stores save their weird shit particularly for this season. And by *weird shit*, I mean amazing vintage they are too dumb to know is worth anything.
5. If there's a flaw, ask for a discount.
6. Loiter until they push the new stuff out onto the floor. I found two Chanel jackets for $8 each that way—they never even made it onto the racks.
7. As always, cash is king.
8. Throw up peace signs and click your heels when you leave with three trash bags of clothing!
9. If cash is king, *Febreze is queen*.

Words belong to
those who use them
only till someone
else steals them back.
/
Hakim Bey

32

Qualities of
a Capricorn

December 22–January 20

You're a compulsive, cheap-ass
bastard, and maybe a little
depressing, too. You also happen
to be hilarious.

holiday 2014.

THE GIRLBOSS FOUNDATION

SOPHIA AMORUSO

34

ROSELI ILANO,
ILANO
ilanodesign.com

The idea for the Girlboss Foundation came about when I was writing my first book, *#GIRLBOSS*. Philanthropy is something relatively new to me—maybe it's because I was so busy hustling for myself and my team, maybe it's the only-child syndrome—who knows? But as I looked around to see what causes I felt passionately about, I found that while there were many, none seemed to hit home like supporting female creative entrepreneurs.

In 2014 we launched the Girlboss Foundation, an initiative that awards grants to women in creative fields who are building businesses. To date we have given more than $90,000 to women across the country. Here you'll meet a few who inspire me every day.

What is a Girlboss to you?
A Girlboss owns her power, a power that is generous, affirming, and inspires others to imagine the possibilities. A Girlboss dreams big and goes big, putting in the work behind the scenes that nobody sees.

Tell us about your business.
I started ILANO because I want to innovate sustainable, ethically produced textiles that create jobs that empower women. We are able to pay our partners seven times their national minimum wage. The steady work and living wages have had a direct impact on the lives of the artisans and their families.

How has your business changed since you received the grant?
As a one-woman operation, I was able to hire a part-time employee, which has changed our workflow tremendously so I can spend more time in the design studio.

Any advice for up-and-coming Girlbosses?
There are times when your mind will be your worst enemy, and getting sucked into the cycle of negative thinking can be your biggest hurdle. Take time every day to look in the mirror and recognize your power, creativity, and talent. Remind yourself why you do this and what you have to say. Nobody has your unique voice, spin, and story—and that is your secret weapon.

DEENA DREWIS,
NOUVELLA
nouvella.com

What is a Girlboss to you?
A Girlboss got to where she is by defying convention. But there's also precision, a clarity of vision, a measure of fearlessness (which can sometimes look like recklessness), and the capacity to metabolize adversity like it's a gross but healthy snack. She wakes up without an alarm clock and doesn't think twice about using the men's room if she really has to pee.

Tell us about your business.
Nouvella is an independent press dedicated to novellas, which are works of fiction that are longer than a short story and shorter than a novel. They're designed to be stashed in your back pocket and read wherever you go.

How has your business changed since you received the grant?
The grant lifted me out of the uneasy state of needing to put every book we print on a credit card. It gave me the breathing room to start thinking about other elements of the business. After receiving the grant, we went on to raise another $25K through a satirical Kickstarter campaign that was sort of poking fun at mainstream publishing while spreading awareness about Nouvella; this was the brainchild of a marketing team I'd hired with the grant money. Your operation starts to resemble a real business, and you suddenly think, This is good! I can do good things with a little operating capital!

Any advice for up-and-coming Girlbosses?
I'm a big-time introvert who has a hard time getting out there to kiss babies and shake hands, and I'm probably patient to a fault. But I think you have to find ways that these—let's call 'em "nontraditional business skills"—work to your advantage. My obsession with detail makes for a slow process, perhaps, but it's also a huge part of what makes the books special. If you're not out there constantly networking because that's not your thing, find the people you really want to connect with and make it genuine. Be appreciative of others and return favors. If you're told you need to do more or be different, consider what impact that has on your original vision. Growth is good, but sometimes protecting your original idea is equally important.

SOPHIA AMORUSO

35

winter 2008.

PIECES DE RÉSISTANCE

- ☐ Black leather jacket
- ☐ Denim jacket
- ☐ White T-shirt
- ☐ Vintage rock tee
- ☐ High-waisted black jeans
- ☐ Shit-kicking ankle boots
- ☐ Black eyeliner
- ☐ Red lipstick
- ☐ A sneer
- ☐ A smile

met my husband in 2002. a great amount of whimsy for a young mind.

i heard this album for the first time when i

Chapter 2

TYRAN-NOSAURUS REX

—

A BEARD OF STARS

"WIND CHEETAH" // HER WITH MOON-TRODDEN PLOW — HERDS OF AFRICAN COWS — GRAZED ON HER BEAUTY — FRAGRANT AND PALE — YOUNG ONCE YOUTHFUL STILL NOW — MUSE TO THE WILLOW AND PLOUGHED — FIELDS

ARCHED WITH
ORCHARDS — BLOOMS
OF THE STARS —
DAY WHIPPED HIS
BLACK DRAY — OPAQUE
ORPHAN OF RING
MYRRH COATED
RIDER — GUIDER
HUSBAND TO MATRON
THE KING — STREAMS
OF YELLOWY MUD

ON LOS ANGE-LES

Spring 2011 .

L.A. gave me legs in more ways than one. I moved here in vintage wide-leg polyester pants and months later was busting out my gams for the first time since I was fourteen. When the sun is beating down on you through your bedroom window, it's a little hard to lie around being depressed—this city springs you into action like no other. I hike. I walk. I love the little birds that live outside. I eat clean! . . . because it's kind of hard to crave takeout chicken tikka masala in 80-degree weather. It's not a city that you can gauge by standing on its sidewalk—you have to exist here for some time to really grasp what L.A. is all about.

As much as everyone complains about the traffic, L.A. is a great place for introverts: You get to be alone from Point A to Point B and avoid the psychic garbage that gets thrown your way on city sidewalks in places like New York or San Francisco. And anyway, driving is just another excuse to listen to Girlboss Radio, right?

SOPHIA AMORUSO

43

Portrait of a GIRLBOSS

SOPHIA AMORUSO

44

DJUNA BEL

STYLIST & FASHION EDITOR
@djunabel

—

The first time I saw Djuna, she was on eBay. She was all of six feet tall, modeling vintage for Mama Stone Vintage, a competitor of mine at the time. I thought she was an angel. Half a decade later, I wound up in a backyard with her on the Fourth of July and the rest is history that includes a lot of pizza.

What do you want to be doing in ten years?
Sitting on a beach with a piña colada.

First job?
I was a grocery bagger at an organic foods store in Santa Cruz, California.

Did you always know you wanted to be a stylist?
As soon as I found out that it was an actual career, I pursued it with all my heart and soul.

Style icon?
Jane Birkin, David Bowie, Nina Hagen, Betty Catroux.

Favorite piece of clothing?
A leather jacket that belonged to Jimi Hendrix.

Dream score?
A Paco Rabanne chain mail dress.

What are you excited for when you wake up in the morning?
"Sex in the mornin'." Oh wait . . . I mean, sometimes.

What are you most grateful for?
My friends and family and the opportunity to live the life I want.

If you weren't doing what you do today, what would you want to be doing?
I would be on that show *Hoarders*.

Album or song on repeat?
I'm not a creature of habit. My obsessions change daily. Right now "Rio" by Duran Duran gets me up in the morning.

Dream client?
Prince.

What's the best thing about what you do?
I only work with people who I love.

What do you absolutely detest doing but have to do?
Driving.

Proudest moment?
Driving on the freeway.

What's next for you?
If I told you I would have to kill you.

Weirdest thing about you?
What isn't weird about me?

Biggest piece of advice for aspiring Girlbosses?
Surround yourself with a network or people who you trust and are inspired by and don't be afraid to ask questions.

LEANDRA MEDINE

FOUNDER OF MAN REPELLER
@leandramedine

—

Leandra is so capable it scares me. She's whip-smart, hilarious, and knows exactly what she wants. To top it off, she's the quintessential millennial style icon. How one human can possess so many qualities has had me baffled since we met.

How did you start your company?
By setting up a URL with Blogger, which was not yet owned by Google at the time.

What are you excited for when you wake up in the morning?
Making new stuff.

What are you most grateful for?
Health.

While we're asking questions like that, what's a Man Repeller?
Whatever you want it to be, really, considering the parameters of confidence and female independence! But I don't want to put it in a box.

What was your first job?
I was a receptionist for a summer at a plastic surgeon's office on Park Avenue.

Do you have a style icon?
New York.

What do you want to be doing in ten years?
I don't really know. I think I'm finally coming to terms with the fact that it's okay that I don't know.

If you weren't doing what you do today, what would you want to be doing?
I would WANT to be doing what I do do, if that makes sense.

Album or song on repeat?
That one about the cheerleader. It makes me want to dance.

What's the best thing about what you do?
Affecting people in a positive way, or helping them figure shit out that can be as simple as what kind of shirt to wear. That is cool.

What do you absolutely detest doing but have to do?
People management—I have realized it takes a lot of self-confidence and -assurance to feel like you are appropriately positioned to tell other people how to act or do their jobs. I'm not sure if I'm there yet.

Proudest moment?
Every time I get to see my team succeed.

What's the weirdest thing about you?
I lie to people about being allergic to bees to justify how I react in their presence.

Biggest piece of advice for aspiring Girlbosses?
Lean into the moments when you feel most vulnerable and really take stock of how you're thinking—from those moments always emerge really interesting change.

What's next for you?
The rodeo.

1970s Saint Laurent.

You are precisely as big as what you love and precisely as small as what you allow to annoy you.

/ Robert Anton Wilson

THIS CLOSET LOWERED
THE VALUE OF OUR HOME
TO THE TUNE OF ONE
ENTIRE BEDROOM.
CLOTHES PAID FOR
ALL OF IT, SO IT'S MORE
LIKE A SHRINE.

My favorite piece of furniture.
1930s italian vanity with
curved purple mirror!

THIS IS THE ROOM AROUND WHICH EVERYTHING CENTERS, WHERE WE ROUGHHOUSE WITH THE DOGS AND DRINK OUR MORNING COFFEE. IT'S WHERE WE SIT BY THE FIRE ON THE RARE LOS ANGELES NIGHTS WHEN IT'S COLD ENOUGH FOR THAT TO MAKE SENSE. LAST NEW YEAR'S EVE, MY FRIENDS AND I WROTE DOWN HABITS THAT WE WANTED TO DIE WITH THE YEAR BEHIND US AND BURNED THEM AFTER READING THEM ALOUD TOGETHER.

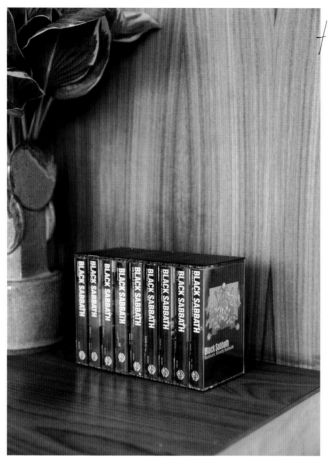

the black sabbath tapes were
a gift - a good one!

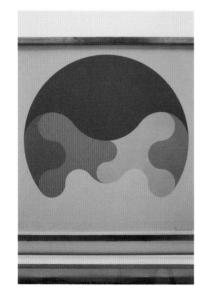

i found this vintage print in
a secondhand store in soho.

the monk sculpture was my yia yia's.
yia yia is greek for grandmother.

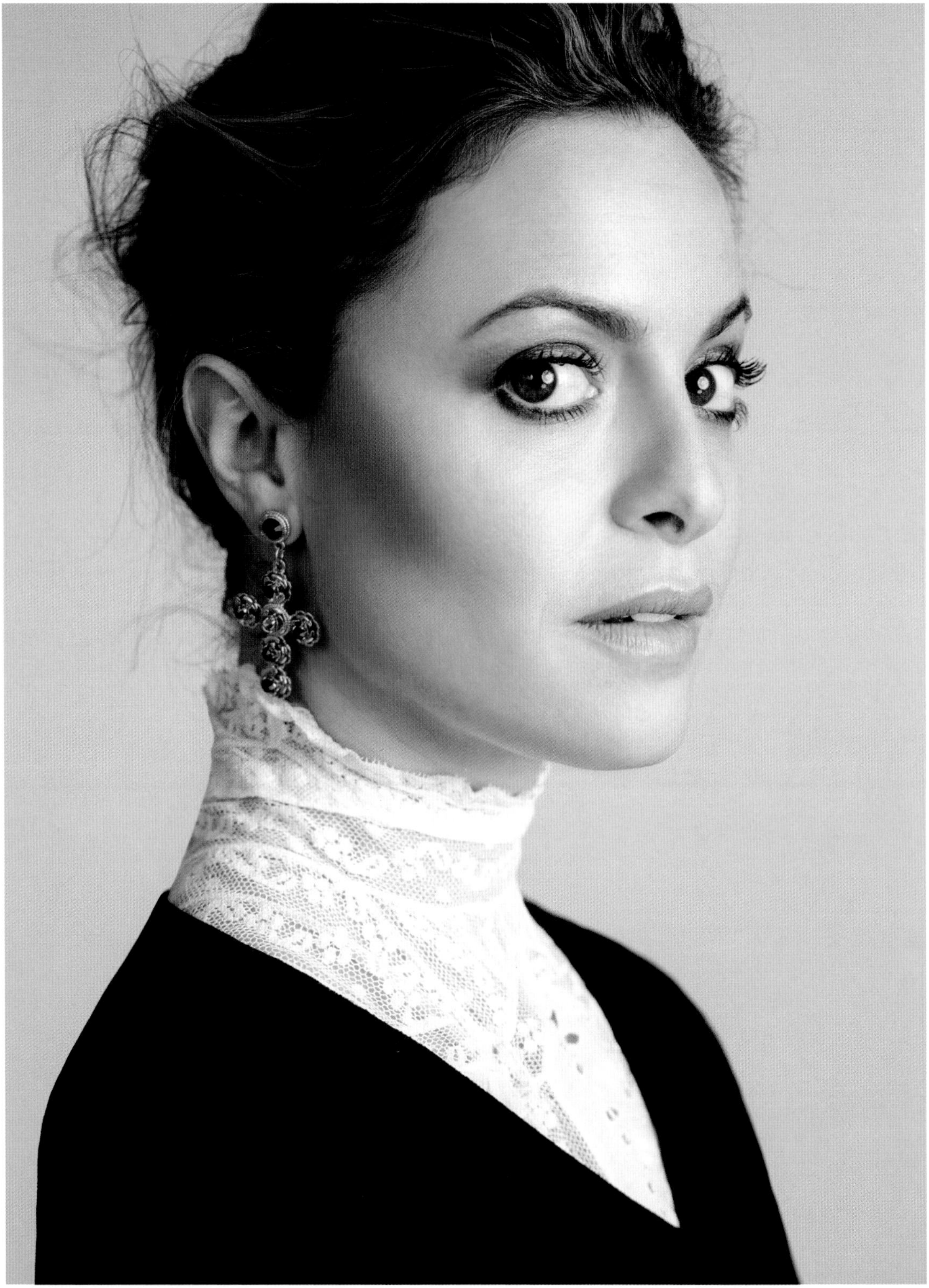

nasty gal earrings.

When in doubt, be extreme.

/

Genesis Breyer P-Orridge

Don't worry about people stealing your ideas. If your ideas are any good, you'll have to ram them down people's throats.
/
Howard Aiken

Qualities of an Aquarius

January 21–February 19

You really do want to make the world a better place, and you're loyal as fuck—but now you just need to show up.

fall 2012.

Daydreaming

subverts the world.

/

Raoul Vaneigem

POISON IVY

Kristy "Poison Ivy Rorschach" Wallace, together with her longtime partner, Lux Interior, was the band the Cramps, known for a very special type of kitschy punk rock, drawing their influences largely from 1950s horror films. Check out the YouTube video of them performing at the Napa State Mental Hospital. Pure gold.

Bad Bitch of MUSIC —

Boys like the things they do to seem real hard like it takes a lot of strength to control them. But I tell you, guitar playing's not hard. It doesn't require any great strength or some male brain pattern. In fact, it's sort of feminine. That's why I wish more women would play guitar, because there'd be more variety in the sound of rock music.

/

Poison Ivy

SOPHIA AMORUSO

61

HOW TO WAKE UP HAPPY EVERY MORNING

1. Plant flowers outside your bedroom
   that attract hummingbirds.
2. If that fails, get a poodle.
3. If that fails, get three. I did.

. . . and for Christ's sake, go to bed!

HOW TO GO COMMANDO

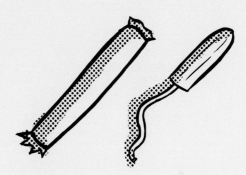

1. Regardless of the time of month, use a tampon.
2. Tuck the string in.
3. No panty lines, no laundry!

this record changed my life. an anthem in eight parts that's dripping in confidence.

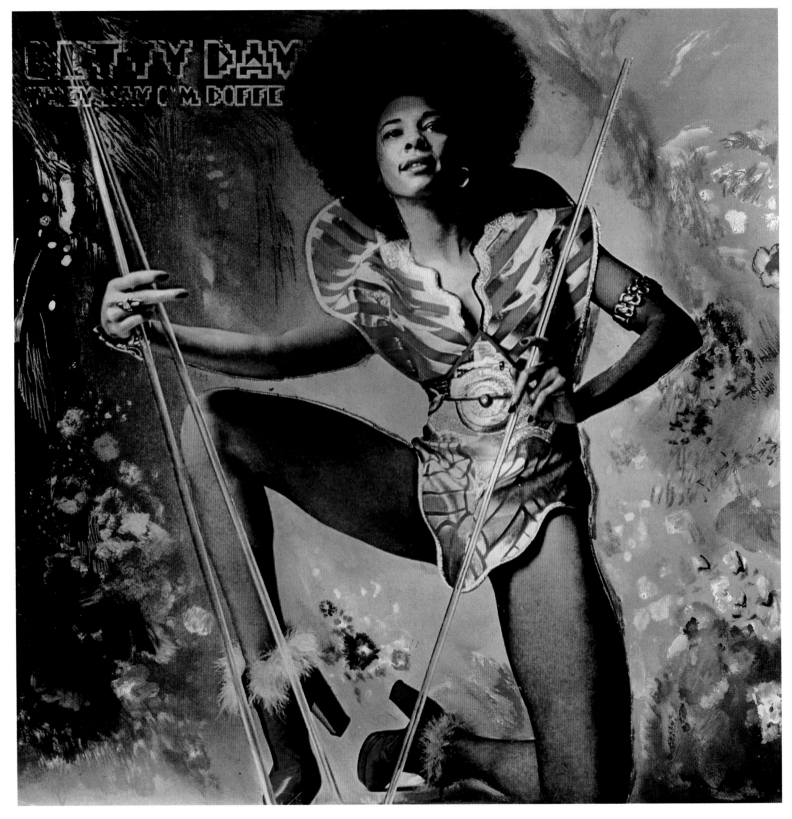

Chapter 3

BETTY DAVIS

—

THEY SAY
I'M DIFFERENT

"DEDICATED TO THE PRESS" // HEY NOW EXTRA EXTRA HAVE YOU READ ABOUT ME— THEY SAY I'M VULGAR— AND SOME PEOPLE CAN DO WITHOUT ME — WELL ALL I CAN SAY IS IT'S SUCH A SHAME—WHY DO THEY BLAME

FOR WHAT I AM [...] THEY SAY I STICK OUT MY TONGUE— QUITE LECHEROUSLY WELL I REALLY DON'T KNOW WHAT THEY'RE TALKIN' ABOUT—I JUST CAN'T SEEM TO KEEP MY TONGUE IN MY MOUTH

Portrait of a GIRLBOSS

AUDREY GELMAN

FORMER POLITICAL
CONSULTANT, CURRENT FOUNDER
& CEO OF THE WING
@audreygelman

—

Audrey and I met at a *Marie Claire* luncheon in
New York during which we learned about power
poses. It was instantly apparent from the moment we
met that she was poised and incredibly smart. When
I learned she also liked Celtic Frost, I almost proposed.

How did you get started?

I became a hard-core political nerd at an early age, and it was always my dream to work on campaigns, especially in New York City where politics can be even more rough-and-tumble than in Washington. I learned more about how to make tough gut calls on the fly and how to accomplish a goal—no matter how daunting—from working in government and on campaigns. I also got to work for elected officials I admired and on issues that are meaningful to me, specifically, pay equity, choice, flex time, and supporting entrepreneurship and small businesses. Campaigns are more like start-ups than people realize—you have to construct a message, recruit a team, raise money, plan a field program, and create a movement overnight. So although I didn't go to business school, I actually feel my ten years in politics prepared me better than anything could to found my own business.

College: Good idea or bad?

Good, ultimately. But it's a system that needs to be modified, updated, do I dare say disrupted?

Why?

I dropped out of college to work on Hillary Clinton's campaign in 2008 and it was the best decision I ever made. But I ultimately finished my degree and am glad I did. I think the traditional model of the liberal arts college is becoming less and less compatible with younger generations. The first real reason for that is cost—it's far too expensive, and it saddles young people with debt for decades. I was always leaving school for internships, real-world experience, to travel and get out of the bubble. It felt too small for me, and I was bad at making friends. But I look back, and it's where I met my political mentors, and it's where my relationship with my best friend was solidified, and I saw some hippies doing shit I'll never forget, so for those reasons, it was worth it and you should finish college.

In our time together, it's surprised me that the most buttoned-up girl I know knows more about obscure punk and metal than most longhairs. What were those formative years that influenced you the most musically?

I grew up listening to thrash metal, black metal, screamo, hardcore, nü metal, and going to shows from around age twelve and on. I was always really focused on doing well in school, succeeding, being driven in my academic and professional careers, but going to shows was a huge part of my identity. My first boyfriend wore corpse paint and sang in a black metal band. I learned how—as a thirteen-year-old, 95-pound, and 5-foot-tall girl—to navigate mosh pits, thrashers, identify who my friends and protectors were, avoid creepers. It gave me incredible street smarts I use on an everyday basis. To this day, when I walk into a show, I immediately feel understood, accepted, and at home in the same way I feel totally insecure and freaked out when I walk into a fancy party.

Weirdest thing about you?

I have tattoos inspired by/dedicated to both the New York Mets and rapper Cam'ron (*Let's Go Mets* in my inner lip and *Killa* in script on my right elbow).

What is a #Girlboss?

A Girlboss is someone in control of her own narrative, who makes the impossible possible and who pays it forward to other women every chance she gets.

What are you excited for when you wake up in the morning?

I just got engaged, and I feel deep gratitude for waking up each morning with a partner who makes me laugh, supports me, and troubleshoots with me. I wake up most excited to hear about his dreams and tell him mine.

What do you want to be doing in ten years?

Having the same friends, being a mom, feeling real serenity, achieving professionally what I need to to put up with as little bullshit as possible, and feeling surrounded only by people I trust and love.

What are you most grateful for?

Having a totally awesome mom.

If you weren't doing what you do today, what would you want to be doing?

Probably a private detective, some kind of forensic detective, because of my obsession with true crime.

What was your first job?

Babysitting and working at a jewelry store in SoHo called GirlPROPS. The owner was a five-hundred-pound woman with a teardrop tattoo on her eye, and they fired me because they caught me studying for my SATs.

Who is your style icon and why?

Lee Radziwill, no contest. Elegance, attitude, pluck, not ever giving a fuck.

Album or song on repeat?

The Game ft. Drake's "100," Bikini Kill's "In Accordance with Natural Law," Terror Squad's "Lean Back," Gorgoroth's "Funeral Procession."

What's the best thing about what you do?

I get to be creative and stand up for myself and the things I believe in.

What do you absolutely detest doing but have to do?

Fund-raising and convincing men to invest in you as a woman under thirty years old is a challenging and unpleasant task, but you meet people in the process who are true blue.

Proudest moment?

Winning the 2013 primary against Eliot Spitzer on behalf of my former boss and mentor Scott Stringer was a big one—we came from behind to win from being twenty points down, being outspent two to one, and running against a former governor with national name recognition. We were supposed to lose. It took grit, resourcefulness, and three months of zero sleep, but we pulled it off because we had a great candidate and a great team.

What's next for you?

I'm founding my own company, a club for women called The Wing, inspired by my own experience as a way-too-busy woman forced to change in Starbucks bathrooms and in the backs of cabs. It's a home base for women with showers, permanent lockers, hair and makeup, rooms for naps, meetings, and pumping if you're a new mom. We're creating something that's shockingly never been done—a "room of our own" that men have had access to for centuries where you can refresh, gather, connect, create relationships, and treat as home base as you zigzag through your day. Our mission is to make women's lives easier, and I could not be more excited to launch it.

Biggest piece of advice for aspiring Girlbosses?

First one in, last one out. Read everything. Make connections with other women and help them when you can. Don't take no for an answer. Figure out your way around any obstacle.

SOPHIA AMORUSO

69

GRACE JONES

Born in Jamaica, Grace Jones was raised in an extremely devout Pentecostal household—in fact, her great-uncle was a Pentecostal bishop and wouldn't allow her to perm or straighten her hair in any way, so she cut it all off. Things changed, though, when she moved to New York, became a model, and then became a disco sensation, with club hit after hit before transitioning her sound into New Wave. While everything she did turned to relative gold, Grace Jones had a totally original, envelope-pushing performance style and sensibility that's often emulated. Fun fact: She also starred in *Conan the Destroyer* with Arnold Schwarzenegger.

Bad Bitch of MUSIC —

When I perform onstage
I become those male
bullies, those dominators
from my childhood.
That's probably why it's
so scary, because they
scared me.
/
Grace Jones

In the U.S. you have to be
a deviant or die of boredom.
/
William S. Burroughs

72

Qualities of
a Pisces

February 20 – March 20

You're *probably* psychic. You're also
probably really easy to manipulate.

summer 2015.

DREAM COLLABORATORS

1. The Virgin Mary
2. Joan of Arc
3. Mary Magdalene
4. Bianca Jagger
5. Marie Antoinette
6. Cleopatra
7. Yoko Ono
8. Medusa
9. Michele Lamy
10. Betty Davis
11. Patty Hearst

winter 2016.

If you don't have
a plan, you become
part of somebody
else's plan.
/
Terence McKenna

les vallizes dénudés was on heavy rotation when i founded nasty gal.

so fucked up. so good !

Chapter 4

LES RALLIZES DÉNUDÉS

—

'77 LIVE

夜、暗殺者の夜 // とても深い夜まるで誰かを殺したみたい—何がお前の飢えを満たす—誰かがお前を夢に見るだけど前は誰をも夢見ない—何がお前の飢えを満たす沈黙の鳥は飛び去た夜の言葉は溶け落た—誰もお前がとどまることを望んで

はいない黒い恋人達はすべてが死に絶えた岸辺にたどりく―すでに黒い烙印を刻みつけられた―お前の両手に血の川を渡り虚無の―滴を飲み干した時お前に最初である名前が名付けられるだろう―お前は俺の傷口俺は誰かを殺すだろう―やさしい暗殺

ON
FEAR

holiday 2015

As I was writing this book, I realized that I have been living in a state of fear. My own private hallway, with doors opening to fear and paranoia on either side and two nice big French doors at the end swinging open to the ultimate nightmare for any entrepreneur: *paralysis.*

That shit is so not me. But the more you have, the more you have to lose. It's a double-edged sword. Have I become the stiff suckered into believing that the things around me are a reflection of who I am? Or is it not possession but the fact that I finally put a stake in the ground and built something of value, something I'm rightfully scared to lose? Do I have perspective, now, truly, for the first time since starting the business, or am I just getting old and staid? Have I let my accomplishments and toys define me, or is that an excuse I'm using to shirk responsibility in an effort to remain "free"?

I'd like to say that this feeling is specific to entrepreneurs, but it's not—it's just the feeling of having things you care to lose. The creeping inertia of identity, possession, attachment, and buying into your own goddamn story. I'm pretty sure the word for that is *ego*. But the things that create these tensions are also some

"The creeping inertia of identity, possession, attachment, and buying into your own goddamn story. I'm pretty sure the word for that is *ego*."

SOPHIA AMORUSO

83

of the best things you can do with your life—they will push you to invest in yourself and the people, things, and ideas you care about. If you're doing that, you're doing the right thing. Get attached. Stay attached. Just don't forget to keep evolving.

I am fighting hard to engineer predictability into my life as much as possible without becoming a total schmuck. To be on time. To have a routine. To make Nasty Gal soar to unseen heights while keeping my feet on the ground and making the difficult decisions that come with trying to run a healthy business.

But let's be clear: Business isn't everything. What I truly fear is the prospect of people I love getting sick. Or my poodles getting eaten by coyotes. Or that I was spoiled by Nasty Gal's early success and won't do everything I can to build an awesome life for myself and my family— that I'll sleep through the alarm clock that is each new day and eventually hate myself for fucking it all up.

And then there are the basics: I'm scared of heights, spiders, eating things that may cut the top of my mouth, and, well, generally, the future.

holiday 2014.

CHERIE CURRIE

SOPHIA AMORUSO

86

Currie became the lead singer of the teenage girl band The Runaways when she was fifteen (she was spotted by Joan Jett at Sugar Shack in Hollywood)—she quit when she was seventeen, had a solo career, and starred in *Foxes* with Jodie Foster. These days, she's a chainsaw artist (and she wrote the must-read *Neon Angel*).

Bad Bitch of MUSIC —

"Cherry Bomb"

Can't stay at home,
can't stay at school
Old folks say, ya
poor little fool
Down the street
I'm the girl next door
I'm the fox you've
been waiting for

Hello, Daddy,
hello, Mom
I'm your ch-ch-ch-
cherry bomb
Hello, world,
I'm your wild girl
I'm your ch-ch-ch-
cherry bomb

Someone told me
to get a life.
"I've had several,"
I replied.

#WWGBD

Power's not given to you.
You have to take it.
/
Beyoncé

Qualities of an Aries

March 21–April 20

You have too much energy and you're
an impatient asshole.

fall 2014.

OUR DESIGNS

92

The Nasty Gal label was born in 2012. After selling only vintage and a dozen or so other brands, it was our first opportunity to dream up anything we wanted—then wear it. There is nothing more gratifying than witnessing an idea take shape and seeing it come to life. To this day, the thrill of finally having our name on a clothing label is not lost on me. Our entire team is obsessed with vintage: We scour personal archives and vintage collections from around the world looking for those lightbulb design moments that we can then make uniquely our own. Vintage is in our blood.

our incredible design team at work.

OUR STORES

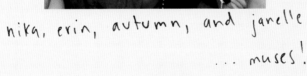

nika, erin, autumn, and janelle ... muses!

We opened our first Nasty Gal store on Melrose Avenue in L.A. in late 2014, and our second just a few months later in Santa Monica. The fitting rooms are surrounded by glass on all sides, with one-way mirrors on the doors, which means you can see out but we can't see you. The sales floor is lovingly called the *dance floor*, and our team members are called *muses*, because they are more than stylists—they inspire me, our team, and our customers every day.

vintage jewelry on display.

How do you make your lover think about another girl?

A: Talk about her incessantly.

i brought this
insane mirror
back from a
paris flea
market.
so disco!

no skateboarding on the sofa!

recorded in the 70s but played on a loop at LaGuardia airport at one point during the 80s. So calming.

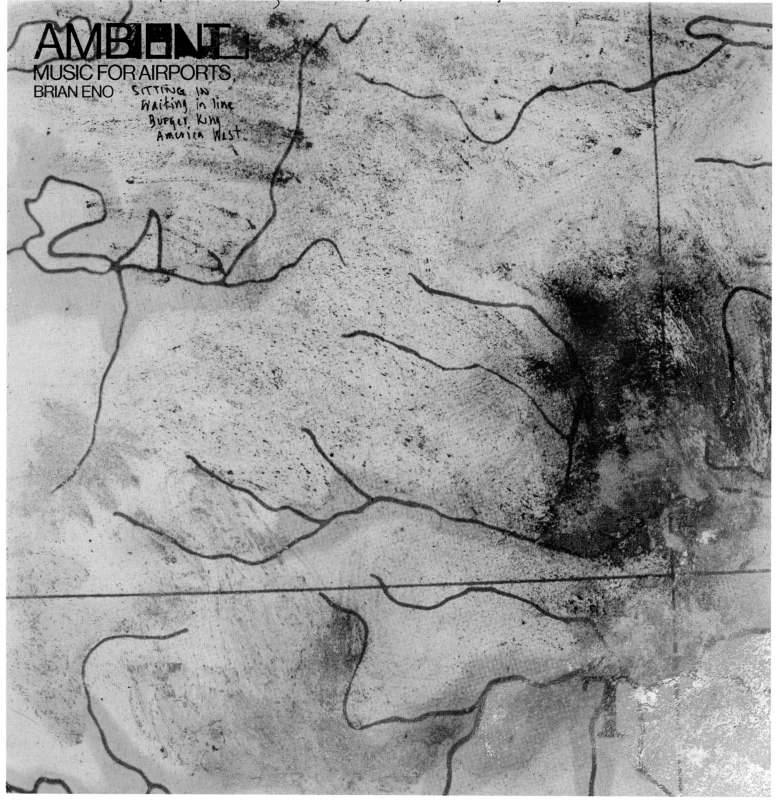

Chapter 5

BRIAN ENO

—

AMBIENT 1:
MUSIC FOR AIRPORTS

ON
LETTING
GO

fall 2012.

One time when I was a teenager I went over to this cute guy's house after eating way too much pizza. As soon as I arrived, my stomach started to hurt, and I could tell it was going to be the runs. I would rather get in my car and drive home than stink up the poor guy's bathroom, so I hopped in my 1991 Honda Civic hatchback and zoomed down the street to the nearest liquor store. I made it into the place, face white as a ghost, and asked if I could use their restroom. They told me it was for employees only. So I jammed my way back down the road, holding in god knows what until I found a gas station. I screeched in, tumbled out of the car, and it was like step, step. . . . *fraaaaaamp*. The pure foam just came pouring out like projectile buttvomit, filling my brown corduroys. As I sat in the black upholstered driver's seat, it came in uncontrollable waves until it was done. The twenty-minute drive home was the longest drive of my life, sitting in the self-respect quicksand that was my own liquid turd.

BOMB DEVILED EGGS
Hard-Boiled Egg, Mayo, Dill, Salt
Done.

104

Don't go around saying the world owes you a living. The world owes you nothing. It was here first.

/ Robert J. Burdette

70s hand-studded denim jacket

COFFEE TABLE BOOKS
THAT WILL MAKE YOU LOOK
INTERESTING

1. *THE BAD SON*
BY HARMONY KORINE

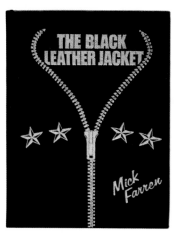

2. *THE BLACK LEATHER JACKET*
BY MICK FARREN

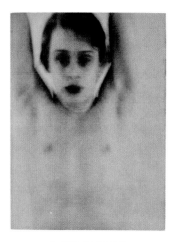

3. *FIORUCCI, THE BOOK*
BY EVE BABITZ

4. *MADEMOISELLE 1 + 1*
BY MARCEL VERONESE

5. *FROM HERE TO THERE:
ALEC SOTH'S AMERICA*
BY GEOFF DYER AND SIRI ENGBERG

fall 2014.

Portrait of a GIRLBOSS

108

CHRISTINE LAI

COFOUNDER & WOMEN'S DESIGNER FOR UNIF
@cornilikeit

—

UNIF was one of the first brands we ever sold.

How did you start your career?
It started out as a side passion project with my partner, Eric, while we both had other jobs. After a lot of hard work, sweat, and tears we were able to make it into our careers.

Did you go to college? Would you recommend it? Why?
I went to FIDM [Fashion Institute for Design & Merchandising] for fashion design, but I really don't recommend it. A simple Adobe Illustrator/Photoshop class would've have been enough. It's pretty important to be able to convey your ideas in the computer; so as long you have the vision and technical skills, you're set.

What was your first job?
Pressed-juice delivery girl (before it was a thing) in 2000.

Style icon?
Steve Jobs.

If you weren't doing what you do today, what would you want to be doing?
A filmmaker or photographer.

Album or song on repeat?
4 Da Summa of '94 by DJ Paul and Lord Infamous.

What do you want to be doing in ten years?
I would love to make a feature film one day, so hopefully by then I'll have the time and money to do it.

What's the best thing about what you do?
Best thing about my job is the people I work with. I have such a pleasant and creative team that

it makes being in this industry (which can be really annoying) actually fun.

What are you excited for when you wake up in the morning?
My first cigarette with coffee.

What are you most grateful for?
My UNIF family, including Eric, my partner.

What do you absolutely detest doing but have to do?
Handling the production side of the brand.

Proudest moment?
When we were able to donate $80K to charities last year.

What's the weirdest thing about you?
I make everyone in the office refer to me as Steve. If they call me Christine, I don't respond.

Biggest piece of advice for aspiring Girlbosses?
If you're feeling like you're not good enough, know that you're already ahead of people who think they are perfect and bound to make it. The fact that you can recognize aspects of yourself that need improvement means you've got an eye for success. Always stay stupid and open to learn more. The ones who think they're sooo smart are usually the ones who fail in the long run.

What's next for you?
We just closed escrow on the first UNIF flagship store so developing it into a true UNIF+LA experience will be fun.

ALEX PRAGER

ARTIST & FILMMAKER
@alexprager
—
Alex is an amazing photographer whom I met through a mutual friend and whose smile might be as infectious as the work she produces.

How did you start your career?
I first started taking photographs when I was twenty, after being inspired by a William Eggleston show I saw at the Getty in Los Angeles.

Did you go to college? If so, would you recommend it?
I didn't go to high school or college. I was homeschooled and traveled a lot.

Your sister, Vanessa, is also an incredible artist. Are your parents artists?
There has always been a creative side to my family. Aside from me, the women in my family all draw and paint, and both my grandfather and great-grandfather were photographers.

What are you most grateful for?
My loving friends and family.

What was your first job?
When I was fourteen, I went to Switzerland with a friend for a time and I worked in her family's knife shop. Through that experience I saw a lot of Europe because on the weekends we'd hop on the Eurostar and see nearby countries. It also put Switzerland deep in my heart, where it will always live. There is no happier place.

Do you have a style icon?
My mom in the 1970s and '80s. Snug, high-waisted, straight-leg jeans with a button-down collared shirt. Kind of Katharine Hepburn style.

Who is your favorite photographer?
I have so many! Martin Parr is up there. He's got a strong love for unique characters.

If you weren't doing what you do today, what would you want to be doing?
Maybe I'd try to work with the ballet somehow. My film, *La Grande Sortie*, is one of the highlights of my career. I just find the whole history of ballet so rich. It's very easy to romanticize and imagine myself getting immersed in it.

Who or what would you love to shoot but haven't had the chance?
I would love to shoot a chase scene.

What kind of camera do you use?
Contax 645, and I shoot on Kodak 400 film.

How do you feel about the fact that with smartphones, everyone is a photographer? Do you agree?
I agree! It makes for more beautiful images in world, and social media makes them more accessible. It's a win-win situation.

Album or song on repeat?
Deerhunter, *Microcastle*.

What's the best thing about what you do?
I enjoy it so much and I think it makes others happy, too.

What do you absolutely detest doing but have to do?
I hate doing the dishes. Luckily, I cook a lot, and the deal is that when I cook I don't have to do the washing up.

Proudest moment?
Right now it's *La Grande Sortie*. I worked with an *étoile* ballerina named Émilie Cozette. It was a powerful experience for me to tell a story using dance.

Biggest piece of advice for aspiring Girlbosses?
Follow your gut. Everyone has her own voice—you just have to learn how to trust yourself.

SOPHIA AMORUSO

109

NINA HAGEN

Born in East Berlin, Nina Hagen was an opera prodigy as a child before going on to become the "Godmother of Punk." She joined the band Automobil before going out on her own. (Giorgio Moroder produced two of her albums.) She has a lot of theories about UFOs and aliens, and sang about them repeatedly—apparently she spotted a "cosmic ship" in Malibu when she was pregnant with her daughter, Cosma Shiva.

Bad Bitch of MUSIC —

I once had a dream and this one familiar god, who was probably one of my master teachers, said, "You should not worry about being on the charts. That's not important."
/
Nina Hagen

...to free us from the expectations of others, to give us back to ourselves—there lies the great, the singular power of self-respect.
/
Joan Didion

Qualities of a Taurus

April 21–May 21

Your devotion to life's creature comforts is admirable; your jealousy, greediness, and inflexibility...not so much!

holiday 2012.

TIPS ON NEGOTIATING

114

· You blow it the second you drive up in an expensive car, so just don't.
· When in doubt, wink.
· It's easier to negotiate for things other people don't want.
· Have cash on hand in case you're dealing with someone who is comfortable evading taxes.
· Bundle, bundle, bundle!
· Go so low you insult them a little, but never a lot.
· Leverage is everything: Are there other opportunities waiting in the wings? On the flip side, can you offer things in addition to cash? No blowjobs or family heirlooms.
· Comparison shop!
· Be willing to walk away.
· If you aren't in a position to walk away, try the above and if you fail, agree to their terms and, for Christ's sake, withhold the tears until you are alone.

HOW TO WRITE
A THANK-YOU NOTE

1. First, be prompt. Thanking someone too late is something I do far too often, and it really takes the wind out of your efforts.
2. Get some stationery with your name on it.
3. Draw a line through your last name—that means it's a casual note, not that you're putting a hit out on yourself.
4. Use a fancy pen. I prefer the Sakura Pigma Micron variety.
5. Congratulations, you're an adult.

cosi, our middle
poodle. she's a
real clown.

OUR BEDROOM WAS INSPIRED BY A PAIR OF VINTAGE SUEDE SHORTS.

brass sculpture by
chris habib.

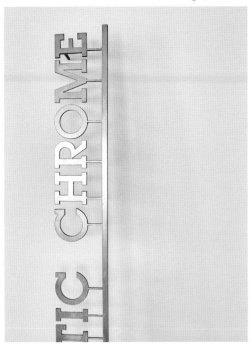

my pin collection.

Kate, my best friend,
made the drawings on the
left. She's a grad
student at UCLA.

the best of his albums - play it   all the way through - no stopping!

ROXY MUSIC

Chapter 6

ROXY MUSIC

—

COUNTRY LIFE

"A REALLY GOOD TIME" // THERE'S A GIRL—I USED TO KNOW — HER FACE IS HER FORTUNE—SHE'S GOT A HEART OF GOLD — SHE NEVER GOES OUT MUCH — BUT BOY—WHEN SHE DOES — THEN YOU KNOW — SHE'S GOT

NO MONEY—WELL, MAYBE A DIME — BUT SHE KNOWS WHAT SHE'S WORTH — AND THAT'S THE REASON WHY — SHE'S GONNA MAKE IT — SHE'S GOT WHAT IT TAKES — YOU'LL APPRECIATE THAT— SHE'S PROBABLY LATE

ON CONFI-DENCE & HUMILI-TY

You know what makes everyone confident? PCP. Just kidding. Don't do that.

I haven't always been confident. There was definitely a time in my life when I couldn't focus beyond the thoughts ricocheting around in my head: Are my hands in the right place? Am I weird? Are they onto me? In the world that I travel in often these days, I will never quite feel like I belong—like I'm as smart as the company I keep.

Listen: I feel like a loser a lot of the time. Like I'm doing what I can until someone figures out that I shouldn't be doing anything at all. I think that's what those in the entrepreneurial world call *impostor syndrome*. If you're a true specimen of a narcissist, you will never experience this. And if you set the bar super low for yourself, you're also in luck! But for the rest of us with hopes, dreams, and aspirations, it's normal.

Here's the thing: I've been overly celebrated because I'm a girl. Because I told a wild, and true, story about how I came up in the world with no degree and figured it out. But living up to my own hype fucking

"Confidence
+ self-doubt
+ capability
+ self-reflection
= humility."

SOPHIA AMORUSO

125

terrifies me. The day that accomplishments like mine are no longer headline news is a day I hope I'm alive. But that doesn't mean I shouldn't celebrate myself. You can celebrate yourself, love yourself, and be confident while remaining humble. Just be careful not to buy into your own dogma. And don't call yourself humble, because that's just weird.

Confidence+self-doubt+capability+self-reflection=humility. Cultivate your talents, but don't let them become your identity. That will breed confidence. Find out if you've earned your confidence by taking a hard look in the mirror and throwing some insults in your own direction. Does your argument hold up? Keep going. Hone your craft over those ten thousand hours, and once you're capable as fuck, you'll know it because the world will respond. And make sure to stop and reflect on who you are, what you are doing, and what you are becoming as a result of your choices. We become the sum of what we spend our time doing and who we spend time doing it with.

At the end of the day, confidence is really a choice. It's a little bit like a muscle. You have to choose to use a muscle to keep it strong. And then you can flex it in those moments of feeling a bit overwhelmed by your surroundings. Shrinking doesn't get you very far. Don't be psychic Swiss cheese. Don't let those invisible darts others send your way pass through you. See the dart and just be a happy, confident, solid piece of Tillamook cheddar. And always mutate consciously, my friend.

fall 2012.

MEIKO KAJI

128

Known for her work playing outlaws, samurai assassins, and delinquents in obscure Japanese movies and exploitation films from the 1970s, Meiko Kaji is most loved for *Lady Snowblood*. She sang the theme song for the movie, too, which was used in *Kill Bill: Vol.1.*

Bad Bitch of CINEMA —

On a dead morning,
a burial of snow falls.
The howling of a stray
dog and the sound of
geta [wooden clogs]
break the silence.
I walk with the weight
of the heavens on my
mind.
/
Meiko Kaji,
"Shura No Hana"
("Flower of Carnage")

Belief is the death

of intelligence.

/

Robert Anton Wilson

Portrait of a GIRLBOSS

132

GWYNETH PALTROW

**ACTRESS, COOKBOOK AUTHOR
& FOUNDER & CHIEF CREATIVE
OFFICER OF GOOP**
@gwynethpaltrow

—

I met Gwyneth through a mutual friend. I wound up at her house for a birthday party and she told me how much she loved *#GIRLBOSS*. What I really love is her thick California accent.

First, and most important, do you use public restrooms?
Not my favorite, but yes, obviously. I am a germophobe, but I'm working on it.

What kind of toilet paper do you buy for your home?
Cottonelle. It should probably be something recycled, but I am a sucker for soft toilet paper.

How has your work life changed since you became a mother?
I essentially changed careers. I find it hard to be away from my kids. I want to raise them myself, but it's hard on an acting career. When I do do it, I make sure they know that I do it because it is important for me as an artist to be who I am. Otherwise, I am home working on the website, which I also love. It presents a whole other set of challenges.

What surprises people most about you?
My dirty sense of humor, probably.

What has been the hardest part of building Goop?
Scaling while remaining true to what we are. It makes the process slower.

What are you excited for when you wake up in the morning?
Coffee. And sex. Can I say that?

What are you most grateful for?
I am most grateful that I know and like myself. I no longer suffer fools, mince words, or am ashamed about any aspect of myself.

My self-respect was hard-won; I really didn't get it until I was forty.

You didn't finish college. Does that bother you? Do you think you'll ever go back?
It doesn't bother me for two reasons. First, I graduated from a school in NYC when I was seventeen called Spence that genuinely prepared me in a way I could have never anticipated and was totally unaware of at the time. It was an all-girls school that taught me how to see things from all angles, to be precise in thinking, and that imbued me with a deep curiosity. That leads me to the second reason: that curiosity has continued to further my education. I think I have accidentally given myself an executive MBA. Well, almost.

What is a Girlboss?
A Girlboss is a woman who is integrated to the point that she is fearless and therefore able to execute on whatever it is she wishes to execute on.

What was your first job?
My parents always made me have an after-school job growing up. Not sure about the legality, but my first job was at age eleven at Penny Whistle Toys on Madison Avenue. It's no longer there, so that Girlboss can't get in trouble. I have always had a job, pretty much.

Who is your style icon and why?
Honestly, any woman who has a clear and individual sense of style stemming from the fact that she knows she is beautiful.

If you weren't doing what you do today, what would you want to be doing?
Retiring? Or doing a musical on Broadway.

Album or song on repeat?
The National, *Trouble Will Find Me.* Alt-J.

What's the best thing about what you do?
The best thing about what I do is that I get to push boundaries.

What do you absolutely detest doing but have to do?
Helping with homework. I'm the absolute worst version of myself.

Proudest moment?
There is a reason that everyone who has kids answers this in the same way. It's because when your kid surmounts some personal obstacle, makes a deep connection to someone, gets complimented on their manners, plays a chord on the guitar, whatever it is, your body basically breaks apart with pride. It's insane.

What's the weirdest thing about you?
There are so many weird things about my life. One time someone asked me if I was me, and if I would take a picture with her while I was peeing in a (public) bathroom.

Biggest piece of advice for aspiring Girlbosses?
You can totally fucking do it.

What's next for you?
A martini.

I used to think dancing was the worst invention ever.
How dorky: publically gyrating to sounds. Like a baby.
I couldn't bring myself to do it until I got a job doing it—
as a go-go dancer—fake ponytail, raised plinth, and all.
For some reason, dancing became fun, perhaps because
I was making money doing it. So I guess you could say
I learned to dance in front of a crowd.

Oh, and sorry, DJs: There's nothing better than an
empty dance floor.

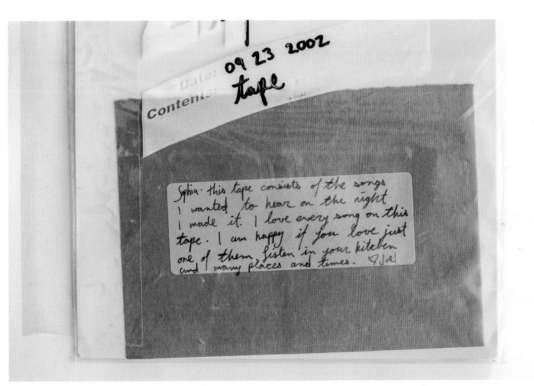

a mix tape my husband made me in 2002.

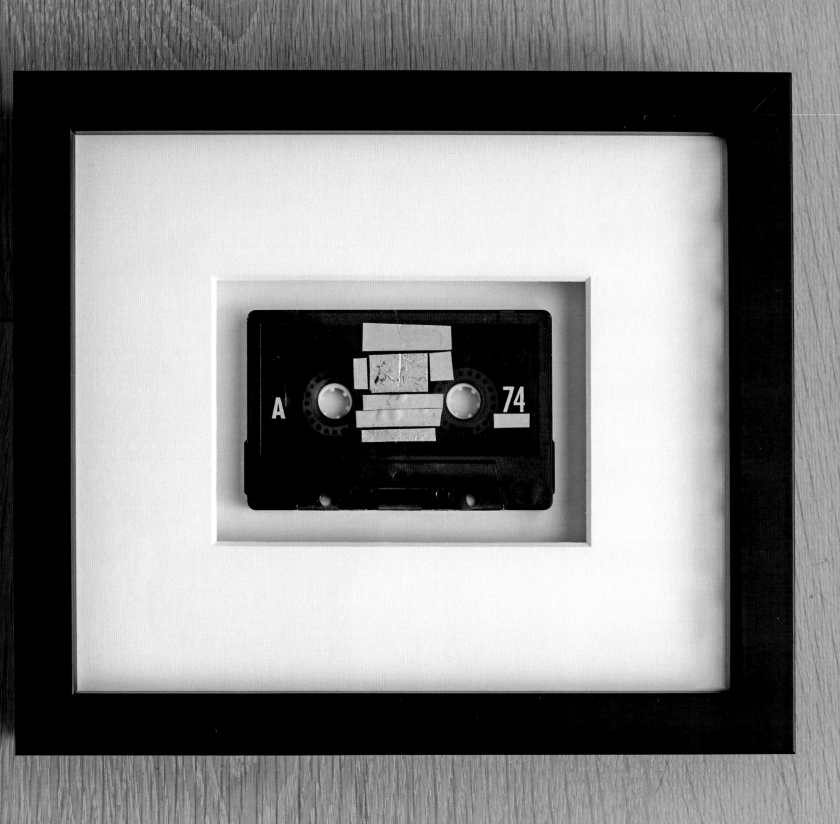

WEDDING PLAYLIST

Ara Koufax: "Brenda"
M.ono: "Holding Back California"
Mirror People: "Kaleidoscope (Psychemagik Remix)"
Fonda Rae: "Heobah"
Slimline: "You Can Dance"
Lily Ann: "Going Crazy"
Donna Summer: "I Feel Love"
Giorgio Moroder: "From Here to Eternity"
ELO: "Turn to Stone"
Sade: "Couldn't Love You More (Vin SOL & Matrixxman Remix)"
HNNY: "No"

Marcus Marr: "Pleasure Moon"
Andy Hart: "Epsilon Girls"
Al Kent: "Born This Way"
Shit Robot: "Work It Out (Todd Terje Remix)"
Robin S: "Show Me Love"
Wildbirds & Peacedrums: "Fight for Me (Manuel Tur Remix & Dixon Edit)"
Paul Simon: "Diamonds on the Soles of Her Shoes (Amé Remix)"
Desireless: "Qui Sommes-Nous"

The trouble with some women is that they get all excited about nothing—and then marry him.

/

Cher

holiday 2014.

ON
BALANCE

As Oscar Wilde said, "Everything in moderation, including moderation." I'd agree with that, but for me the lesson is in excess, not moderation. So I moderate my excess. Moderately. With an attention span the length (if it can even be defined by its length, rather than its lack thereof) of an eyelash, I have to constantly remind myself to choose less whenever possible.

Everyone talks about balance. About doing it all and having it all. About being a working woman in a relationship, or a single mother, or a busy single lady who's trying to date, and how hard it all is. It *is* hard. But life is hard and that's the most normal thing we can possibly accept. Balance hasn't existed since the fabled Garden of Eden, but quite honestly, I'm glad we get to wear clothes, so thanks, Eve.

SOPHIA AMORUSO

141

HOW TO DRIVE LIKE A GIRLBOSS

1. Before using the brakes, let the weight
   of the car slow it down.
2. Brake, gas, brake, gas is a terrible idea,
   and for the passenger, it's like being driven
   around in the trunk of an NYC cab.
3. Never use two feet to drive an automatic.

HOW TO PARK LIKE A GIRLBOSS

1. Turn off the radio.
2. Roll down your car windows.
3. Listen for starting cars.
4. If it's cold, look for the hot exhaust of running cars.
5. Voilà, you're as neurotic as I am!

The main thing is that the main thing stays the main thing.
/
Stephen Covey

Qualities of a Gemini

May 22 – June 21

You talk a great game—and it's legit fun to listen to—now just pretend like you were actually intending to follow through.

summer 2012.

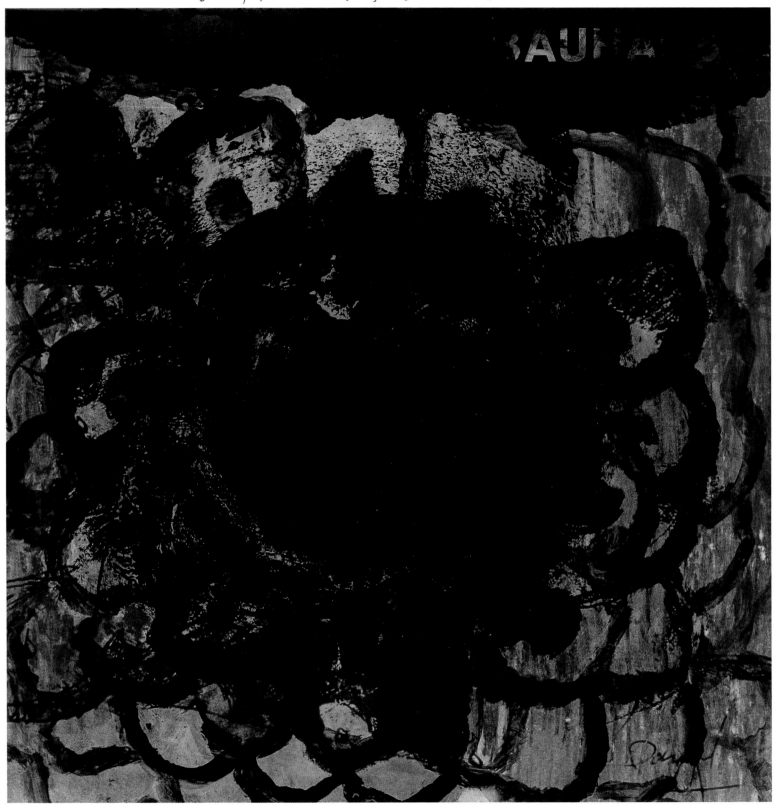

check out "the passion of lovers."

BAUHAU

—

MASK

"KICK IN THE EYE" //
SO I BEGAN THE
CROSSING — MY
THROAT BURNED DRY
— SEARCHING FOR
SATORI — THE KICK
IN THE EYE —
I AM THE END
OF REPRODUCTION
GIVEN NO
DIRECTION — EVERY

CARE IS TAKEN —
IN MY REJECTION
— KICK IN THE EYE
KICK IN THE EYE
KICK IN THE EYE KICK
IN THE EYE —
EVERY CARE IS
TAKEN — WITH MY
REJECTION — AND
MY ABDUCTION —
FROM MY ADDICTION

holiday 2014.

ON FRIEND CHURN

Be so good the
ideas you discard
are other people's
aha moments.

#WWGBD

When you hit thirty, something weird happens with friendships that I call *friend churn.* You lose touch with your friends. Then, like a whirlpool, you cycle your way up to the top again, and when it's meant to be, you get back in sync. Or . . . not. When you're young and have a crew who drinks, goes to school, or simply fucks off together, there is little room for dissonance besides the random disagreement over who doesn't throw down when the bill comes.

When you hit thirty, it's the time that careers are either taking off or people are still building them, going back to grad school, or have chosen to have no ambition at all. It becomes more and more difficult to coexist among people who want less for themselves than you want for them. Thirty is the age when you want friends who have something to say when you ask, "What's new?"

There are only a few people in my life who knew me when—and they're the only ones who can truly help me get a grip when it all starts to slip. We are all in different places in our lives, careers, and relationships, but what we acutely have in common is that we are all malleable. We are always learning, growing, and trying new things without judgment of one another.

There are a lot of things holier than business, and you can bet your ass that friendship is at the top of that list for me. All I ask in return is that you agree—not with your words, but with your actions. I fired a friend during the writing of this book, which sucked, but sometimes you're just not on the same wavelength and it's nobody's fault. It's the risk we take by investing in people. Some investments just don't have the same return as others and some returns really are diminishing or nonexistent. But that's the nature of the beast—the best of the best will always come back around.

at eighteen, saving tons
of dough and having zero
boyfriends by cutting my own hair.

PAM GRIER

Though nominated for a Golden Globe for Quentin Tarantino's *Jackie Brown,* Grier's work in 1970s blaxploitation movies like *Foxy Brown* and *Coffy* is even better. She's often credited as the first female action star. As the poster for *Coffy* explains, she's the "baddest One-Chick Hit-Squad that ever hit town!"

Bad Bitch of CINEMA—

I do a movie
once every four
years and they
call it a comeback.
/
Pam Grier

Lack of charisma
can be fatal.
/
Jenny Holzer

I do not know how to teach
philosophy without becoming
a disturber of the peace.
/
Baruch Spinoza

Qualities of
a Cancer

June 21 – July 22

You're always looking out for
everyone else—and, you know,
letting the world get you down.
Figure out how to let the past be
the past and kill the grumpiness.

fall 2014.

because i stink.

prized possession:
original set of
fiorucci stickers!

a very pretty room where very disgusting things happen.

Portrait of a GIRLBOSS

PEGGY NOLAND

ARTIST
@peggynoland

—

Peggy Noland is social media on legs. With an iconic style all her own, she is someone who I've admired for years. She has the perfect Madonna gap, has dressed the likes of Rihanna and Miley, and turns heads wherever she goes.

How did you start your career?

There was a tiny storefront available in Kansas City, and after a few years of consigning my clothing to local boutiques, I had the crazy idea that I knew enough to open my own shop, and put in an application for the space. Well, long story short, I didn't know enough, looking back, but it didn't matter. I learned by doing and knew that I was committed to myself and my dreams. It worked, and that's still my ethos today. I don't think I have ever done anything the "right way," meaning having had the proper education or training for any of my endeavors. From owning a business, to sculpting, to painting cars, I either just started and met each problem as it came—or watched YouTube tutorials. :)

Did you go to college? If so, would you recommend it? Why or why not?

I applied to FIT [Fashion Institute of Technology] and didn't get in, so that was sign enough for me. I opened a store instead of going to college and used the money I would have had to spend on tuition on rent and inventory. I had a separate full-time job for the first six or so years that I had my shop open in order to pay rent. College is such an individual decision, based on what you'd like to do, your level of personal motivation, and even your personality. Although I don't have a degree, the Kansas City Art Institute asked me to teach in their Fiber department while I was living in K.C. Initially, I took the job because I needed the money, but fell in love with teaching. Being around students who are eager to learn, sharing ideas, and helping to develop trade reminded me of why I began making clothes in the first place. So would I recommend college? Yes! But if someone sees a pathway outside of college that they are excited to pursue, I would also recommend that everyone follow their instinct.

What do you want to be doing in ten years?

The same thing I do today, plus more, more, more! Being in a better position to enable more Girlbosses!

What are you excited for when you wake up in the morning?

Coffee and seeing if my sister-in-law has posted any new photos of my niece, Olivia, and nephew, Graham.

What are you most grateful for?

My family. They have always been behind any crazy idea I had.

What was your first job?

I was a waitress at a nursing house in Independence, Missouri, all four years of high school. A lot of my high school buddies worked there, too, so we have many fun stories to reminisce on, from pranking our boss, to things we won't mention in print!

Your haircut is so iconic. How long has it been that way? Do you have a name for it? Do you cut it yourself?

I have had a version of this haircut for about eight years now! I look back at pictures of myself with a full head of hair and think, What was I thinking?! Although I don't have a name for it, I think it keeps me closer to looking like a video game character, and to me, that's always a good thing. There are certain members of my family who I always wear a hat around to avoid the conversation. And every once in a while, when I get irritated with people staring at my head, I am reminded I am annoyed when people stare, but even more annoyed if people don't!

Do you have a style icon?

Michele Lamy. I recognize, though, that it is a luxury to present yourself to the world in that way.

If you weren't doing what you do today, what would you want to be doing?

I would be an aide to those with mental disabilities. I was doing this type of work for the first six years my store was open, and it's one regret that of mine that I find it hard to run my own business, manage employees, create the product, and still find time to do work that doesn't serve my ego.

Album or song on repeat?

Miley Cyrus & Her Dead Petz!

What's the best thing about what you do?

That I have freedom to explore my ideas. I think about all the genius women who were never in a position to have their writings, painting, ideas, etc., received by others, and it is such a reminder that if we are in a place where we can create and share, we need to act on that.

What do you absolutely detest doing but have to do?

Dishes. I will skip a meal rather than having to dirty a dish.

Proudest moment?

Hitting the ten-year mark with my retail store. I was convinced I wouldn't even make it one year!

What's the weirdest thing about you?

I own only ten outfits.

Biggest piece of advice for aspiring Girlbosses?

Tell yourself YES. That crazy, harebrained, nonsensical idea that just won't go away—that thing that brings you so much joy to think about although you can't really explain why? That's the thing you're on this planet to do.

What's next for you?

Opening a store in L.A. in January and filming a girl-power version of *Pimp My Ride.*

SOPHIA AMORUSO

163

ON REVENGE

summer 2018

Revenge: It's fun to daydream about and even more fun to watch.

Cheap and thrilling in the form of a B movie, but short-sighted and juvenile to act on. In reality, nothing ever ends with an eye for eye. As Gandhi once said, "An eye for an eye only ends up making the whole world blind." If you exact revenge, however minor it may be, you're only inviting more negativity into the world. Put simply: Tit for tat is not the tits. Be better than that. You just don't know what harm the universe will inflict on you for being the petty idiot who rubs someone's toothbrush on the toilet.

I never wanted to
be anything

other than who I was.

/

Kim Gordon

bowie's most tragic sounds. brian eno of "music for airports" produced.

Chapter 8

DAVID
BOWIE

—

LOW

"BE MY WIFE" // SOMETIMES YOU GET SO LONELY — SOMETIMES YOU GET NOWHERE — I'VE LIVED ALL OVER THE WORLD — I'VE LEFT EVERY PLACE — PLEASE BE MINE — SHARE MY LIFE — STAY WITH ME — BE

MY WIFE — SOMETIMES
YOU GET SO LONELY
— SOMETIMES YOU
GET NOWHERE —
I'VE LIVED ALL OVER
THE WORLD —
I'VE LEFT EVERY
PLACE — PLEASE BE
MINE — SHARE MY LIFE
— STAY WITH ME —
BE MY WIFE

BETTY DAVIS

Though largely remembered as (briefly) being the wife of Miles Davis (she's credited with inspiring his electric "Bitches Brew" phase), Betty was the mother of a certain brand of sex-infused funk (and the inspiration for the name of Nasty Gal). While at first glance she looks like just another stunning style icon, her lyrics, and her voice, were anything but typical. She made some real noise.

Bad Bitch of MUSIC —

If Betty were singing today she'd be something like Madonna; something like Prince, only as a woman. She was the beginning of all that when she was singing as Betty Davis. She was just ahead of her time.
/
Miles Davis

Stop telling women
to smile.

#WWGBD

174

Qualities of
a Leo

July 23 – August 22

You're really fun at a party—but
you're also a bossy asshole.

spring 2014.

Silk 1960s indian
print dress.

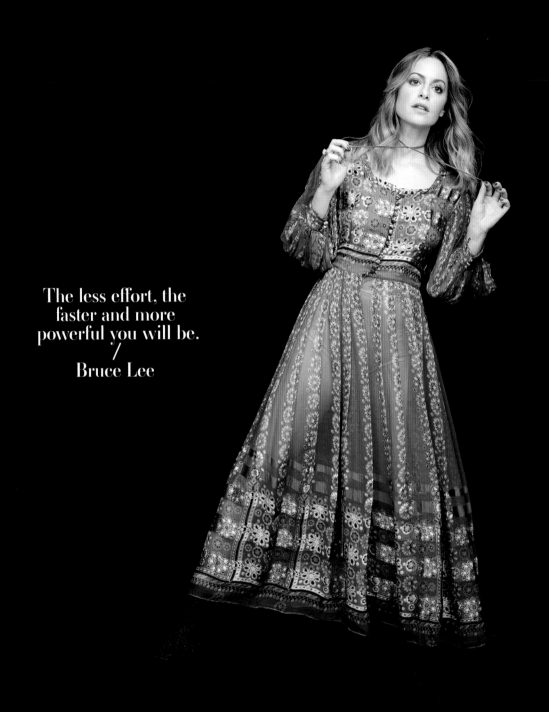

The less effort, the
faster and more
powerful you will be.
/
Bruce Lee

a 1960s mobile phone? the cord inside plugs into the wall - and works!

I just killed a caterpillar.
I didn't mean to do it.

Spring 2003

cryptic mail.

1940s velvet dress

If you're wondering what's wrong with my voice, I just choked on my saliva.

/

Grace Jones

HOW TO GET IN SHAPE FOR A WEDDING

1. Buy a dress one size too large.
2. Have it taken in.
3. Feel good about yourself.

HOW TO
ORDER
A BOTTLE
OF WINE
LIKE
A TRUE
ASSHOLE

1. Look at the bottle like you've seen the label before.
2. Smile and wink to let the sommelier know it's the correct year as you try to remember what the word *terroir* means.
3. Sip said wine like you know the difference between a foyer and a closet.
4. Swish it between your teeth like Listerine.
5. Nod with approval while talking to the person next to you like the sommelier isn't actually there.
6. Send the bottle back after drinking an entire glass.

a super dark country - tinged album.
dipped in weirdo psychedelia.

Chapter 9

THE POPPY FAMILY

—

WHICH WAY YOU GOIN' BILLY?

"THERE'S NO BLOOD IN BONE" // MARIE NOW WALKS, HER LIFE IS SLEEP — SHE NEVER LOOKS ABOVE HER FEET — SHE NEVER SMILES, NOR DOES SHE SPEAK — WHEN JOEY DIED, MARIE WENT MAD — SHE'D GIVEN HIM

WHAT LIFE SHE HAD — SHE'D HELPED HIM FIGHT AND SHARED HIS PAIN — HER VERY BLOOD WAS IN HIS VEINS — BUT THERE'S NO BUT THERE'S NO BUT THERE'S NO THERE'S NO BLOOD IN BONE

holiday 2015.

ON
NET-
WORK-
ING

I used to think that networking was creepy. I think it's a gross word—it's like saying you're going to go out just to increase the size of "your network," which is fucking weird. But these days, I think networking is just another way of saying yes, and I do some version of that now.

I resisted it for a long time because I thought I could solve all my problems without anyone else's help, or that I didn't have anything to learn because my story was different. And yeah, my story is different, but there's stuff to learn from everyone you meet. I've met so many people who are willing to help me out, or give me advice, or introduce me to someone who might be able to give me advice. Just people who are excited to help me solve problems.

Now I try to do the same: I get a lot of satisfaction from it because when you get to help other people, it's good for you, too—it's a break from your own problems, a break from yourself. When there's so much of *you* happening, being able to focus on someone else is really a joy.

SOPHIA AMORUSO

189

Some of the people I've met grew up really wealthy, or went to the perfect school, or have never been an entrepreneur, or have a big job at a big company. I could tell myself I'm not like those people. And while there may be some fundamental differences between us, I learn a lot from people of all kinds and find that I have more in common with them than the "old me" would ever have guessed. I've learned to be more open and less judgmental and found a way to enjoy people because of who they are, rather than the music they like. Thank God, I figured that one out—I'd have no friends today if I hadn't.

holiday 2013.

SU TISSUE

The little-known group Suburban Lawns—part of the 1970s post-punk scene in Los Angeles—put out a handful of records and then disappeared. Su Tissue was never really quoted in the media, though she is credited by her bandmates with coming up with lyrics about genitals and janitors. So, clearly, she was brilliant.

Bad Bitch of
MUSIC —

"Janitor"

I'm a janitor
Oh my genitals
I'm a janitor
Oh my genitals
Oh my genitals
I'm a janitor
/
Su Tissue,
"Janitor"

1970s east west leather jacket and custom Levi's

No one can make you feel inferior without your consent.

/

Eleanor Roosevelt

I love sleep. My life has the tendency to fall apart when I'm awake, you know?
/
Ernest Hemingway

Qualities of a Virgo

August 23 – September 22

You're so totally OCD and analytical that you should run everyone's life; that said, you actually want that job.

holiday 2012.

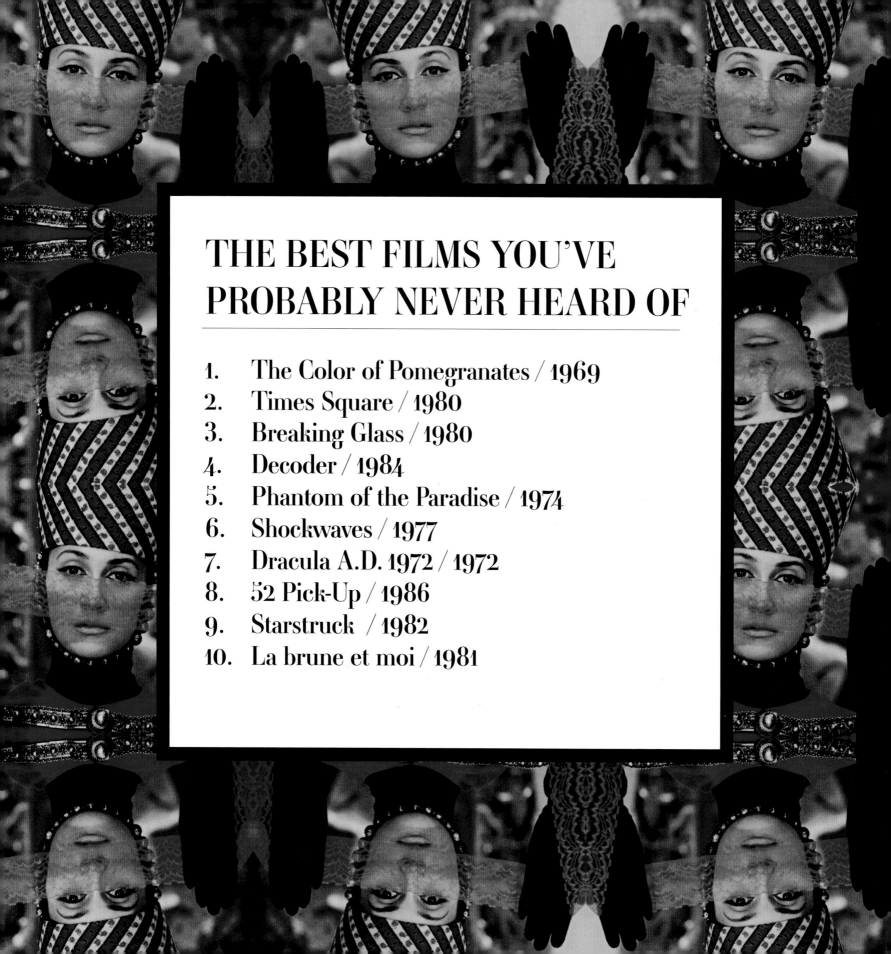

THE BEST FILMS YOU'VE PROBABLY NEVER HEARD OF

1. The Color of Pomegranates / 1969
2. Times Square / 1980
3. Breaking Glass / 1980
4. Decoder / 1984
5. Phantom of the Paradise / 1974
6. Shockwaves / 1977
7. Dracula A.D. 1972 / 1972
8. 52 Pick-Up / 1986
9. Starstruck / 1982
10. La brune et moi / 1981

Portrait of a GIRLBOSS

200

CRYSTAL MOSELLE

FILMMAKER, DIRECTOR,
AND PRODUCER
@crystalmoselle

—

I met Crystal through my friend Jauretsi; both are filmmakers and had worked on a project together. Crystal then went on to win the Sundance Grand Jury Prize for her feature-length documentary, *The Wolfpack.*

What was your first job?
I was a cashier at a burrito spot.

How did you get started in film? Did you always know you wanted to be a director?
I wanted to be a director since I was about fifteen. I had been an actress up until then, but started to feel too self-conscious being in front of an audience. Stepping behind the stage or camera felt more natural to me. I always knew I would come to New York. During art school I produced and shot a documentary on Taylor Mead, which eventually went to the Tribeca Film Festival. After that I started shooting my friend's photo shoots, which led to me directing commercials. The turning point was when I met this group of brothers named "The Wolfpack." This project is what changed everything for me.

Do you have a style icon?
Maybe Janet Jackson meets Stevie Nicks.

Who is your favorite director?
I love the work of Jane Campion.

What do you want to be doing in ten years?
I want to make films, but I am also very passionate about helping people and our planet. So I would like to be doing more of that, too.

What was it like winning the Sundance Film Festival's Grand Jury Prize?
I wouldn't know because I blacked out! It was a real honor and I still can't believe it. Afterward I walked backstage and got my picture taken with Winona Ryder, which was a teenage dream come true.

What are you excited for when you wake up in the morning?
I'm excited to continue to work on all my projects.

What are you most grateful for?
That I get to be creative for a living.

If you weren't doing what you do today, what would you want to be doing?
I think I would be some sort of engineer or naturopathic doctor.

Album or song on repeat?
Darkside or anything by Nicolas Jaar.

What's the best thing about what you do?
The moment when you are so inspired by what you are capturing and creating . . . it feels similar to falling in love. That passion that feels like drugs.

What do you absolutely detest doing but have to do?
I don't really detest doing anything. I do have to say that doing eight months straight of nonstop press for a film is not easy.

Proudest moment?
Finishing *The Wolfpack.* After four and a half years of hard work, it felt good to have something to show that I was proud of.

What's next for you?
I'm writing a screenplay and continuing to work with the boys in *The Wolfpack* on some projects.

Weirdest thing about you?
I don't drink coffee, or any caffeine, for that matter. I am not the biggest fan of live music. I love music and love dancing, I just don't like to stand watching a band.

Biggest piece of advice for aspiring Girlbosses?
Be clear with your vision and what you want to do . . . then follow through. Never give up until you make that vision come to life.

SHEREE WATERSON

CEO OF NASTY GAL, BUT YOU
CAN CALL HER SHERPEE
@nastygal

—

Sheree and I met in a pretty typical way—through a recruiter. However, our work together has become a friendship based in purpose and far beyond typical. I love this woman.

How did you start your career?
By working my way through college at UC Berkeley. I started as a gift wrapper during the holidays at a cool boutique (by the way, I wrap a mean gift). I wanted to become a kindergarten teacher, but I was rejected by Berkeley's Teaching Credential Program and decided to work another quarter in the boutique until I got accepted. I kept getting promoted and, one day, was called to interview at the buying office for a junior assistant buying position in lingerie. My dream was to become the designer sportswear buyer there, and three and a half years later I did.

What is a Girlboss?
A Girlboss is brave and doesn't let disappointments in life get in her way. She's a warrior. She's a manifester.

What is a Nasty Gal?
She's a Girlboss with style.

Are you a Nasty Gal?
Oh hell yes.

Describe your style in three words.
Sporty. Goth. Warrior Princess.

What is leadership to you?
Leadership is providing vision, clarity, coaching—and embodying it all.

What inspires you?
Beauty, adventure (of any sort), humor, collaborating with people to achieve a goal, and experiencing when people get excited. If I can be the spark to other people's flames—if I can ignite passion in somebody and I can see that being unleashed—that fulfills me. I completely geek out over that.

What book would you recommend everyone you know read?
The Four Agreements, A Course in Miracles, The Hard Thing About Hard Things, and *#GIRLBOSS!*

What was your first job?
Being a waitress at Anna Miller's Pies in Concord, California. . . . Cute outfits and I got to yodel! *Yoodolehewhooo.*

What do you want to be doing in ten years?
Teaching, writing a book, advising companies, and traveling my ass off!

Do you have a style icon?
Audrey Hepburn, Grace Kelly, and Chrissie Hynde.

If you weren't doing what you do today, what would you want to be doing?
Climbing Mount Kilimanjaro.

Album or song on repeat?
"Venus in Furs."

What's the best thing about what you do?
Collaborating with smart people and manifesting cool shit.

What do you absolutely detest doing but have to do?
Taxes.

Proudest moment?
My proudest moment is yet to come.

Biggest piece of advice for aspiring Girlbosses?
It doesn't matter what reality looks like to you right now. If you hold your dreams and never let go, those dreams will come to meet you.

What's next for you?
Becoming a spy.

SOPHIA AMORUSO

201

vintage siouxsie + the banshees tee & 80s studded skirt.

There ain't no answer. There ain't gonna be any answer. There never was an answer. That's the answer.

/

Gertrude Stein

CAULIFALAFEL

1. Buy a box of falafel mix.
2. Take some cauliflower florets,
   coat with olive oil, then throw
   into a bowl with falafel mix.
3. Sauté in pan until cooked through
   and nicely brown.
4. Throw onto a tortilla with
   avocado, sprouts, and Vegenaise.

i can listen to dunkelheit over and over.
this guy is sick but the music is genius.

Chapter 10

BURZUM

—

FILOSOFEM

"DUNKELHEIT" // WENN DIE NACHT EINFÄLLT — BEDECKT SIE DIE WELT — MIT UNDURCHDRINGLICHER DUNKELHEIT — KÄLTE STEIGT VOM BODEN AUF — UND VERPESTET DIE LUFT — PLÖTZLICH — HAT DAS LEBEN NEUE — BEDEUTUNG

WENN DIE NACHT
EINFÄLLT — BEDECKT
SIE DIE WELT — MIT
UNDURCHDRINGLICHER
DUNKELHEIT — KÄLTE
STEIGT VOM BODEN
AUF — UND
VERPESTET DIE LUFT —
PLÖTZLICH —
HAT DAS LEBEN
NEUE — BEDEUTUNG

ON INTRO-VERSION (AGAIN)

holiday 2015.

Quiet people, especially women, are often misconstrued as bitchy. I'm not the girl who walks up to you at the party. But I'd love to be.

You'd think that after years of clinking glasses and scoring free hors d'oeuvres I'd have figured it out. Nevertheless, I just can't manage to be the person who trots over to say hello. I don't even know where to start with that conversation. I have a lot of respect for people who know how to do that, though. I feel like I should be that person.

It's not all bad: I've gotten so much better at socializing in general. I can entertain now, which is new. I can ask people questions that take the tension out of a room. I am willing to be the clown who eases everyone into feeling safe. But who am I kidding—I was born the clown.

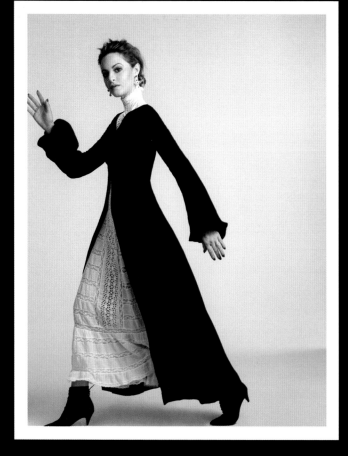

I work from
awkwardness. By that
I mean I don't like
to arrange things.
If I stand in front
of something, instead
of arranging it,
I arrange myself.
/
Diane Arbus

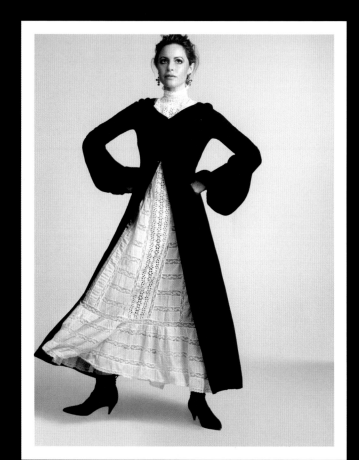

1970s biba jacket + victorian dress.

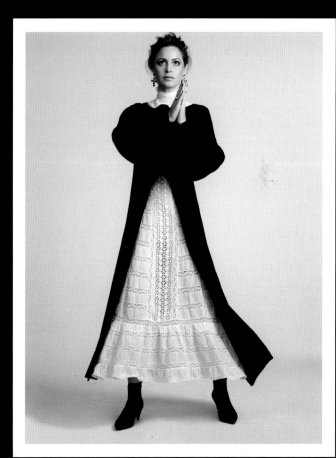

CHRISTINA LINDBERG

214

Christina Lindberg starred in the Swedish exploitation film *Thriller: A Cruel Picture* (aka *Hooker's Revenge* and *They Call Her One Eye*), which would inspire Daryl Hannah's character in *Kill Bill*. She played a kidnapped girl who is chained up and turned into a heroin addict and prostitute by a pimp named Tony (who also slices her left eye). On her rare afternoon off, she learns self-defense and takes her revenge. After this movie, Lindberg opted out of acting, as she was increasingly offered more hard-core films. These days, she edits a Swedish magazine about aviation.

Bad Bitch of CINEMA —

I have never seen most of my films, and probably it is best that way!
/
Christina Lindberg

"The Movie That Has No Limits of Evil! First They Took Her Speech . . . Then Her Sight . . . When They Were Finished She Used What Was Left of Her For Her Own Frightening Kind of Revenge! THEY CALL HER ONE EYE"

SOPHIA AMORUSO

215

HOW TO GET ANYWHERE

1. Act like you own the place.
2. When in doubt, remember that it's better to ask for forgiveness than permission.

THINGS I'VE LEARNED FROM MY HOLLYWOOD TRAINER

SOPHIA AMORUSO

217

1. Walk 14,000 steps a day (I never do).
2. Hollow pretzels exist to rescue your binge dignity.
3. Have three servings of protein a day the size of your palm.
4. Eat fruit with edible skins.
5. Make this healthy pancake recipe:
   Mix 2 cups of dry oatmeal with 4 egg whites. Throw in some raisins, shape into a pancake, and put it in a pan like a pancake. Once "cooked," throw applesauce on top and a cap full of maple syrup. So much fiber. And protein. And I hear it's healthy (see above).

It really is a pity that you can't get into me.

/

Betty Davis

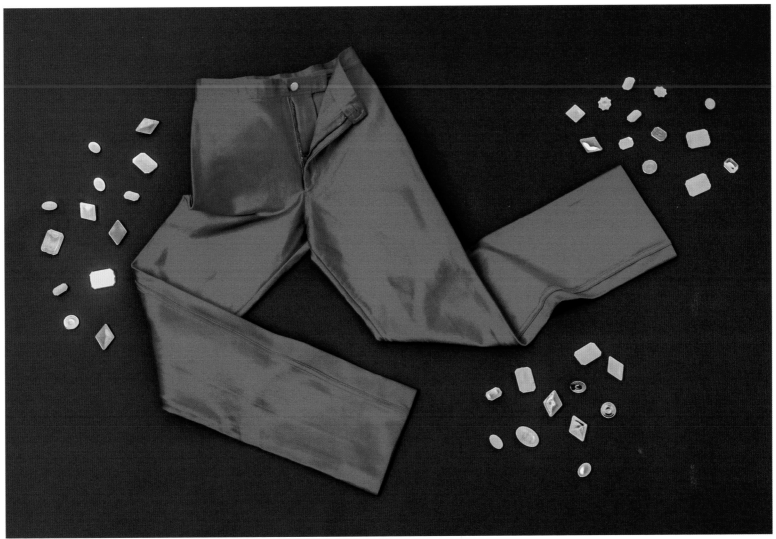

my first memory of buying vintage - disio pants.

FRUITFUL EBAY SEARCH TERMS

"Saint Laurent Yves"   "Jean Paul Gautier"   "Paco Rabbanne"   "Ann Demueldemeester"
"Vintage Channel"   "Emelio Pucci"   "Zandra Roads"   "Bibba"
"Ozzie Clark"   "Junya Whatanabe"   "Norma Kamli"   "Louie Vuitton"

Until you're ready
to look foolish,
you'll never have
the possibility
of being great.
/
Cher

Qualities of
a Libra

September 23 – October 22

You're a big-time flirt and have the
attention span of a butterfly.

fall 2014.

The secret of getting ahead is getting started.

/

Mark Twain

winter 2013.

ON BEING WRONG

Being wrong is blissful. To be wrong is to forge new neural pathways. Being wrong is an adventure. There is nothing more therapeutic than thinking we knew ourselves or how the world works and realizing that we were wrong all along. I almost want to use the word *trippy* here, but I won't.

When I find out I'm wrong, I'm impressed. Accepting that you can be wrong is the genesis of being capable of respecting other people. Consider yourself lucky to have people in your life who can prove you wrong; we should all hope to be surrounded by individuals bold enough to play with the fabric of reality.

SOPHIA AMORUSO

225

Being right and being righteous are two very different things. Being righteous is egotistical. Being right is using what the good Lord gave you. But here's the thing about all of it: There can be many simultaneous truths. You can be right with the wrong people. You can be technically right, but the application is wrong. Or you can be right about something that doesn't fucking matter. Don't confuse your self-worth with being right, because it's a fool's errand—you just have to keep moving.

226

winter 2013.

ON
BEING
RIGHT

PATTI SMITH

228

A Few Things You Might Not Know About Her:

1. She put her daughter up for adoption.

2. She lived in the Chelsea Hotel with Robert Mapplethorpe.

3. She cowrote a play with Sam Shepard and wrote for *Rolling Stone*.

4. In 1977, she accidentally danced off a stage and broke her neck.

Bad Bitch of MUSIC —

Some of us are born rebellious. Like Jean Genet or Arthur Rimbaud, I roam these mean streets like a villain, a vagabond, an outcast, scavenging for the scraps that may perchance plummet off humanity's dirty plates, though often sometimes taking a cab to a restaurant is more convenient.

/

Patti Smith

SOPHIA AMORUSO

229

jarvis cocker makes the most mundane things sound romantic.

ah, the brits.

Chapter 11

PULP

—

DIFFERENT CLASS

"COMMON PEOPLE" // SHE CAME FROM GREECE SHE HAD A THIRST FOR KNOWLEDGE — SHE STUDIED SCULPTURE AT SAINT MARTIN'S COLLEGE — THAT'S WHERE I CAUGHT HER EYE — SHE TOLD

ME THAT HER DAD WAS LOADED — I SAID "IN THAT CASE I'LL HAVE A RUM AND COCA-COLA" — SHE SAID "FINE" AND IN THIRTY SECONDS TIME SHE SAID — "I WANT TO LIVE LIKE COMMON PEOPLE"

ON
LOVE

spring 2014.

With love, I prefer to tiptoe in, look around a bit, and then make a move.

Perhaps it's due to being a child of divorce—but I tend to not let my life be run by emotions. When we're gripped by lust, anger, fear, etc., we can convince ourselves of anything we want to. I prefer to be an eyes-wide-open kind of girl.

As a concept, love is really oversold in our culture. It's intimidating to consider waiting for this extreme moment that's endlessly portrayed in movies, television shows, and romance novels. We've all been sold a dream of long walks, lingering kisses, smelly roses, and life being like an episode of *The Bachelor*. It leaves us hoping and waiting for this thing to hit us over the head and knock us off our chair.

Here's the thing: There are so many different kinds of love, and so many ways to be in love. Love is complicated, continually evolving, and always surprising in its ability to burst and fade. It's fun as shit at the beginning: exciting and crazy and earth-moving, but in reality, loving someone is way more important than being in love. Nobody can live up to the hype that you create for them when you tell yourself that you're madly in love with them. It's a high that can only last for so long before you hopefully settle into something that lasts a lot longer: Real love, marked by affection, and companionship, respect, and most of all, a shared vision.

The people who want it all in a partner are the people who are single forever. They want a best friend, a supermodel, a cheerleader, a comedian, a great co-parent, a provider, the most interesting person in the world, and an excellent party date. Good luck. Do you have all of those qualities? The yin and the yang is never quite as symmetrical as it appears to the naked eye.

236

HOW TO MUTE YOUR POOP

1. Get a wad of toilet paper.
2. Throw it in.
3. POOP.
4. Congrats! You've successfully taken a quiet dump!

SIOUXSIE SIOUX

Born in Bromley, England, Siouxsie—of Siouxsie and the Banshees—
started making music after she went to a Sex Pistols concert as a teen,
then decided to follow them around as a quasi-sidekick as part of
The Bromley Contingent. Before punk became full-on pick, she
epitomized its style, wearing full-on bondage gear. She is one of the
movement's most enduring and loved heroines, and continues to
make music to this day. Fun fact: Siouxsie's father was a bacteriologist
who spent a period of time in the Congo, where he milked venom
from snakes. He was an alcoholic, and died from cirrhosis of the liver
when Siouxsie was only fourteen.

Bad Bitch of MUSIC —

I grew up having no faith in adults as responsible people. And being the youngest in the family I was isolated—I had no one to confide in. So I invented my own world, my own reality. It was my own way of defending myself— protecting myself from the outside world. The only way I could deal with how to survive was to get some strong armor.
/
Siouxsie Sioux

SOPHIA AMORUSO

239

I don't look good in beige.

/

Joan Jett

How wrong it is for a woman to expect the man to build the world she wants, rather than to create it herself.
/
Anaïs Nin

Qualities of a Scorpio

October 23 – November 21

You're an intense motherfucker and you're really good at getting everyone on your side—hellllo, Congresswoman! Now just kill the jealousy.

fall 2012.

COCKTAILS FROM

KIR ROYALE
Champagne, Crème
de Cassis

THE CARMEN SAN DIEGO
Tequila, Cilantro, Lime, Angostura
Bitters, Orange Bitters

THE JUICE BAR
Vodka, Cucumber, Celery
Shrub, Lime

THE STUD
Bourbon, Dubonnet, Bénédictine,
Angostura Bitters

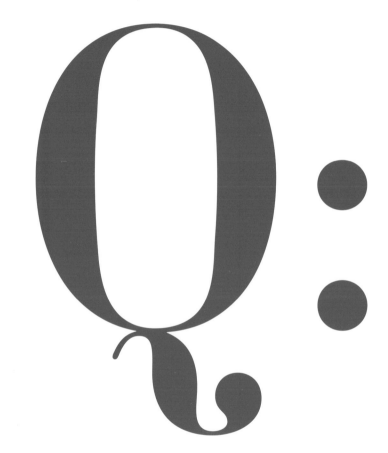

What to demand when you're wearing black in a fancy restaurant?

A: A black napkin.

another dark one! his best album.
    recorded during a time when he was hanging w/charlie manson.

Chapter 12

NEIL YOUNG

—

ON THE BEACH

"REVOLUTION BLUES" //
I NEED A CROWD
OF PEOPLE — BUT
I CAN'T FACE THEM—
DAY TO DAY — I NEED
A CROWD OF PEOPLE
— BUT I CAN'T
FACE THEM — DAY TO
DAY — THOUGH MY
PROBLEMS ARE
MEANINGLESS — THAT

DON'T MAKE THEM
GO AWAY — I NEED
A CROWD OF
PEOPLE — BUT I
CAN'T FACE THEM —
DAY TO DAY — I
WENT TO THE
RADIO INTERVIEW —
BUT I ENDED UP
ALONE AT
THE MICROPHONE

ON
HUGS

fall 2014

When I was in high school, I hung with a bunch of girls who would literally get out of the swimming pool and pee on the lawn when nobody was around. We'd throw dry dog poop at boys, and my one friend could suck air into her butt and fart on demand. We were so gross. And it was so much fun. And then one summer we all came back, and my friends' voices were higher, and they had developed phony lisps, and they started to hug everyone. They got so huggy overnight. Extreme hugginess. Hugs in the morning and during lunch and between classes. And I was like, "Guysss . . . what about farts? And tampons? And all the things we think are funny?"

The hugs grossed me out. That weird display of affection seemed so insincere—and I wasn't about to waste my reach. I would go to live shows in downtown Sacramento and I'd see people I knew, and they'd try to hug me. I'd have to sort of skulk away from them, or stick my hand out for a handshake instead. I tried to save my hugs for times that mattered and people who mattered. I still do. I don't understand the urge to hug someone just because you've met them before. Blame it on the high school girls.

KATHLEEN HANNA

254

Two words: *Bikini Kill*. Based out of Olympia, they were one of the seminal punk girl bands from the 1990s, and Hanna is credited with creating the third-wave feminist Riot Grrrl movement. With her snarky scream leading the way, she has provoked generations of girls to think about their femininity differently. Here's a fun fact: She was born on the same day and place as Tonya Harding. Oh, and she fittingly married a Beastie Boy.

Bad Bitch of MUSIC —

I always tell girls who say they want to start a band but don't have any talent, "Well, neither do I." I mean, I can carry a tune, but anyone who picks up a bass can figure it out. You don't have to have magic unicorn powers.
/
Kathleen Hanna

SOPHIA AMORUSO

255

Portrait of a GIRLBOSS

SOPHIA AMORUSO

256

LIZ CAREY

COMEDIC ACTOR & WRITER
@thelizcarey

—

I met Liz through my friend Galen, whom she was dating at the time. She came over and could have been weird and territorial but instead was warm, friendly, and inquisitive. She put me at ease in my own home. And she's almost as disgusting as I am, so we became fast friends.

How did you start your career?

I started my career modeling and parlayed it into working the red carpet at E!, but I realized I liked making jokes on the red carpet more than asking people who they were wearing. My first comedy job was working on *The Late Late Show with Craig Ferguson*. I would come on and do sketches and act crazy. I caught the major comedy bug there.

Did you go to college? If so, would you recommend it? Why/why not?

I did not go to college. I went to clown school. Just kidding . . . I can't say if I would recommend it because I have no idea what it's like. I was secretly jealous of my friends who went, only because I liked the idea of living in a dorm. I liked the idea of my mom taking me shopping for "dorm furniture" at IKEA. For some reason I will of course pressure my son to go, because it seems like you should go. But he may have other plans.

You're a single mom. How do you, you know, do it all?

I have no idea. *I Have No Idea* seems to be the title of my autobiography and the answer to all these questions? It gets done and some of it does not. I make a lot of lists and I have incredible friends and help while I am working. I never think I am "doing it all"—I am usually thinking, I could do this better. I will say that I have a really easygoing kid who makes life really sweet. Also, kids wake up early so I feel like I have no excuse not to get it done. Though I do seem to spend a significant amount of time at the grocery store in comparison to my single friends.

What do you want to be doing in ten years?

Napping. But after that I hope to be spending more time writing. I would like to have another kid, too? I know that because this one is not enough. I want to adopt one as well. I should probably consider finding a boyfriend along the way, but I have ten years, though, right?

What are you excited for when you wake up in the morning?

My son brings me coffee in bed. Sorry, I don't want to brag, but he does. It's the best part of my day.

What are you most grateful for?

Wow, I am a #Momboss. . . . my son.

What was your first job?

I worked at a fried chicken place in Ohio during high school. My mom thought I was saving for college but I was actually saving up to move to L.A. I had more jobs in high school than anyone on this planet. That could be an exaggeration.

Do you have a style icon?

Jane Birkin.

If you weren't doing what you do today, what would you want to be doing?

I tried stepping outside the comedy world and launched a handbag line. I have to say, it was fun and interesting but I was never more miserable. If I was not creating or being surrounded by comedy, I would be lost. Comedy has always gotten me through my life.

Album or song on repeat?

J Mascis, *Several Shades of Why*.

What's the best thing about what you do?

I play pretend all day.

What do you absolutely detest doing but have to do?

Drink eight glasses of water a day? How is this even possible if you are not near a bathroom all day? I hope there is a Girlboss out there figuring out a solution to this with a magical water pill.

Proudest moment?

Wow, am I this lady? Having my son.

What's the weirdest thing about you?

I have OCD. I don't take any meds for it, but it has its moments— a lot of counting in my head, a lot of checking and rechecking. I sleep with earplugs in every night, though that is not OCD, it's just weird. It would be less time-consuming to compose a list of the normal things about me. I'll stop now.

Biggest piece of advice for aspiring Girlbosses?

Don't quit. I took a break to spend time with my son, and it was a lot harder than I thought it would be coming back into the world of comedy. I am still figuring it all out. There are days when I think, *This is too much*, or I compare myself to other people. Just keep going and going—you will get there.

What's next for you?

I just wrote my first half-hour comedy. Getting that made is what is on the calendar this month . . . stay tuned!

LAURA McLAWS HELMS

FASHION HISTORIAN, AUTHOR, CURATOR, RESEARCHER & DOCUMENTARY FILM PRODUCER. COFOUNDER OF *LADY* MAGAZINE.
@laurakitty

—

Laura and I were Instagram buddies long before we ever met, and then when we did meet, we found out we had mutual friends. She is a vintage hound like no one I've ever known, and looks great in it to boot.

How did you start your career?

I'd always been passionate about historic fashion, but I had figured it was a hobby, not a career. But after working a number of not-great jobs following college, I realized I really had nothing to lose. I decided to go back to school to get my MFA in fashion and textile studies, and everything started to fall into place. While still applying, I met my mentor, the historian Kohle Yohannan, and immediately started working on a show at the Metropolitan Museum of Art's Costume Institute (*The Model as Muse*)—it was a trial by fire, but also instant love.

You wrote a book about Thea Porter. Tell us about it. Why Thea Porter?

I had always been a fan and collector of the London fashion scene in the late 1960s and '70s. When I was doing my master's I realized that, unlike most of her contemporaries (Ossie Clark, Bill Gibb, Zandra Rhodes, and Jean Muir, for example), there wasn't much information available about Thea Porter and no book or exhibition had focused on her yet. I started researching and tracked down her daughter, who gave me access to Thea's business and personal archives. From there, I had more than enough information to write my thesis on her, which led to the book and curating an exhibition at the Fashion and Textile Museum in London. Being given access to an unseen archive is every historian's dream—I am so grateful that this happened with my first big independent project. Thea's

daughter worked with me on the book—writing the foreword and afterword—while the rest of my text covers Thea's life in London, her designs and their inspirations, her place within fashion history, as well as her celebrity clientele. Not only were her designs beautiful and glamorous, but she herself was an immensely interesting and intellectual woman.

Did you like college? Would you recommend it?

I personally love going to school, so I found both my undergraduate and graduate studies immensely interesting. I was lucky both times to be part of small, intensely passionate programs (undergrad at NYU's Tisch School of the Arts for photography, and master's from FIT). It's a wonderful experience being surrounded by such talented people who are as curious as I am. I also worked on my PhD for a year and a half before leaving—I personally missed the class aspect of school and had already gotten a book deal, so I decided it wasn't for me. I learned a lot in that time, but I don't regret leaving at all. School is wonderful, but it has to invigorate you.

What do you want to be doing in ten years?

More of the same—writing (history and novels), and working on documentaries and museum exhibitions, and other fashion-related projects. Hopefully living in the country part-time.

What was your first job?

The summer after high school I assisted an independent

filmmaker—typing scripts, organizing a movie shoot, and managing the production.

What are you excited for when you wake up in the morning?

Opening my eyes to my cats and my boyfriend all cuddled up in bed with me, then going out into my little Brooklyn yard with some hot water and lemon. My schedule is never the same day to day, so I always have some interesting interview or research to look forward to.

What are you most grateful for?

My family's support.

Style icon?

My paternal grandmother, who gave me all of her wardrobe. All my favorite babes: Jerry Hall, Raquel Welch, Joan Collins, Ursula Andress.

If you weren't doing what you do today, what would you want to be doing?

Either writing novels (which I plan to start doing soon) or interior decoration. I also have deep dreams of being a Beatrice Wood–esque ceramicist, clad in silk caftans and living on my family's mountain farm.

Album or song on repeat?

Forever and always, Trespass's *One of These Days* and "Stormchild."

HOW TO BE
AN AGGRESSIVE
PEDESTRIAN

258

1. Collect a loogie in your mouth.
2. Keep the loogie in your mouth.
3. Use the loogie when a car cuts you off in
   a crosswalk. Aim for the trunk—that way,
   they can't see you in the rearview mirror.

HOW TO CHECK OUT OF A FANCY HOTEL

1. Just leave.

Shhhhh. I'm listening
to reason.
/
Pee-wee Herman

Qualities of
a Sagittarius

November 22 – December 21

You'd happily backpack around the
world by yourself. But while you're
out on the road, you should probably
pick up some tact.

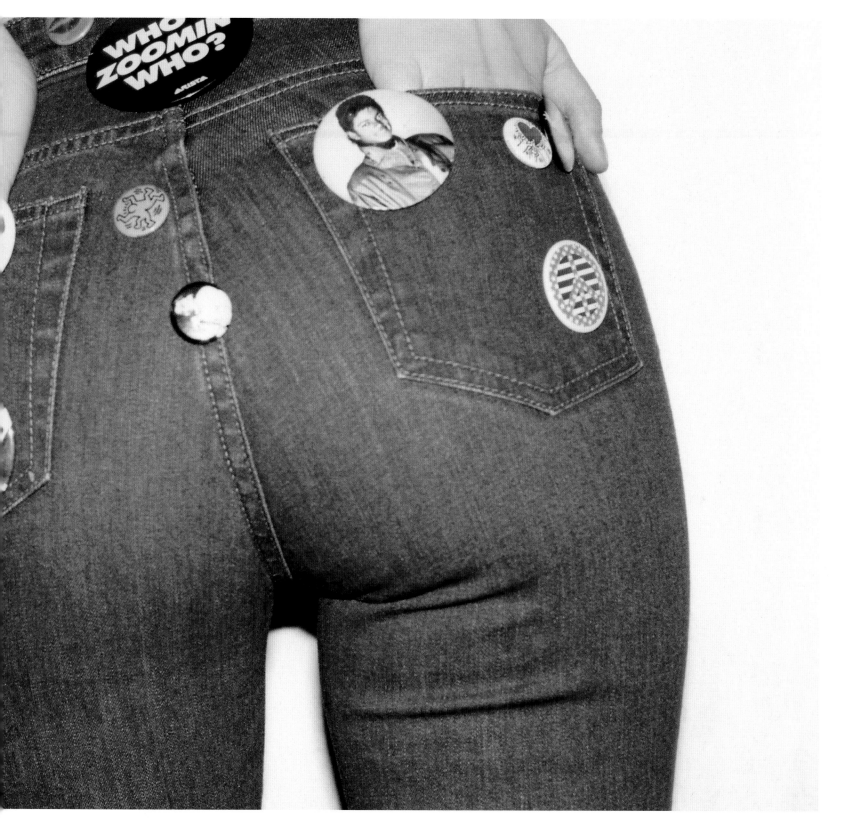

fall 2014.

EXENE CERVENKA

Exene was in the legendary L.A. punk band X—which makes her one of the main driving forces behind the booming punk scene of the '80s. (Fun fact: she co-owned a boutique called "You've Got Bad Taste.") Exene is one of those artists who is a multi-hyphenate: She's a poet, artist, author, freethinker, and conspiracy theorist.

Bad Bitch of MUSIC —

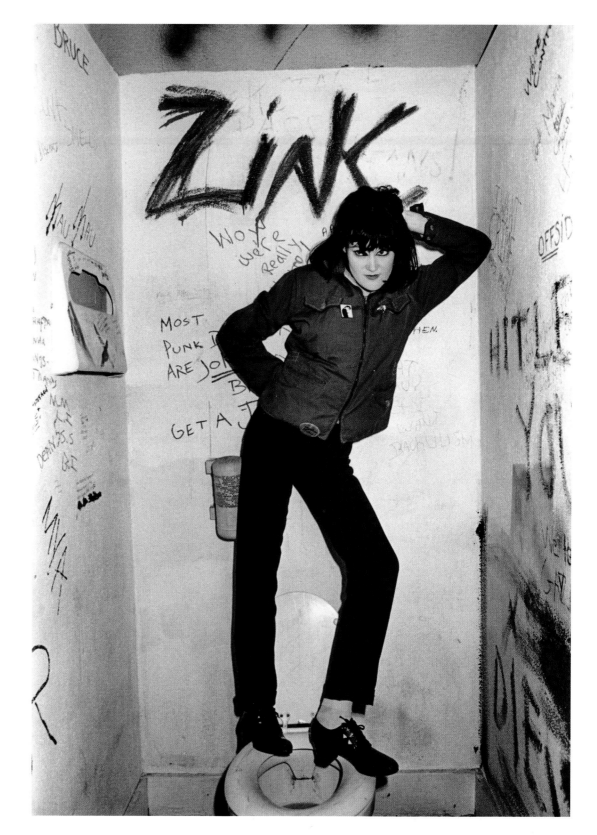

I would not want anyone to try to look like me. My whole point is that I look like myself and you should look like yourself. That's my whole goal in life: to be a freethinker and to help people learn that skill, which we all have innately inside of us. You can only be you. You can't really be someone else.

/

Exene Cervenka

I don't know where I'm going from here but I promise it won't be boring.

/

David Bowie

Credits

Front cover, title page, pages 10, 12, 26, 46, 54, 92, 105, 156, 156, 156, 157, 157, 157, 174–75, 180, 194, 201, 202, 212, 212, 213, 213, 222, 240, 265, back cover: Photography by Chad Pitman.

Pages 1, 36–37, 42, 56, 93, 93, 191, 144–45: Courtesy Nasty Gal.

Pages 6, 22, 24, 24, 25, 48, 49, 50, 52, 52, 52, 53, 96, 97, 97, 116, 118, 119, 119, 119, 135, 136, 153, 160, 160, 161, 178, 178, 179: Photography by Roger Davies.

Page 8: Jan Welters / Trunk Archive.

Pages 14, 38, 64, 78, 98, 120, 146, 168, 184, 206, 230, 248: Kate Stewart. Mixed media on laser prints. katespencerstewart@gmail.com.

Pages 18, 72–73, 76–77, 124, 164, 210, 224, 227: Zoey Grossman.

Page 29: Eve Productions/ Photofest.

Pages 30, 31, 62, 63, 114, 142, 143, 216, 217, 237, 258, 259, 267: Illustrations by Tuesday Bassen.

Pages 32–33, 82, 85, 140, 188: Magnus Unnar.

Page 34: Monica Semergiu.

Page 35: Dana Boulos.

Page 38: © Peter Sanders Photography.

Page 44: Magdalena Wosinska.

Page 45: Krista Anna Lewis.

Page 61: Tony Bock/Getty Images.

Page 69: Billy Farrell/BFA.com.

Page 71: Chris Walter/Getty Images.

Pages 74–75: GAROFALO Jack/ Getty Images.

Page 87: © Chris Walter /Retna Ltd./Corbis.

Pages 90–91, 107, 158–59, 220–21, 252, 260–61: Motoyuki Daifu.

Page 93: Jeff McLane.

Pages 100, 150: Michael Hauptman.

Pages 102, 115, 204–05, 219, 244–45: Stephanie Gonot.

Page 106: *From Here to There: Alec Soth's America*. Published 2010 by the Walker Art Center. Edited by Siri Engberg. Designed by Emmet Byrne.

Page 106: Copyright © by Plexus Publishing Ltd.

Page 106: Taka Ishii Gallery Photography / Film.

Page 108: Derek Perlman.

Page 109: Sally Peterson.

Page 111: © Tony Frank/Sygma/ Corbis.

Pages 112–13, 196–97: Hugh Lippe.

Pages 127, 242–43: Terry Richardson.

Pages 129, 155: Photofest.

Page 132: Steven Sebring / Trunk Archive.

Pages 134, 182, 183: Samm Blake.

Page 137: Playlist by Primo Pitino.

Page 162: Renata Raksha.

Page 173: Guy Le Querrec/ Magnum Photos.

Pages 174–75, 234: Jason Nocito.

Pages 193, 263: Ann Summa.

Pages 198–99: Courtesy of Kino Lorber, Inc.

Page 200: Kava Gorna.

Page 215: Cannon Films/ Photofest.

Page 229: Michael Ochs Archive/ Getty Images.

Page 239: Gus Stewart/Getty Images.

Page 255: Ebet Roberts/Getty Images.

Page 256: Travis Schneider.

Page 257: Paul Maffi.

Acknowledgments

I've written this book during one of the most transitional times in Nasty Gal's history. Ten years has passed since this brand was founded on the spirit of being your unafuckingpologetic self. And today that is how we remain. Everyone who touches our brand is writing our history with me. Thank you, first and foremost, to my team for having fought this uphill battle with me. To anyone who has ever written an email subject line, answered a customer care email, or boxed up a pair of shoes on behalf of Nasty Gal, thank you. Thank you to Sheree Waterson for holding down the fort. And to our customers for giving us all a reason to wake up and stay inspired.

Thank you to my family. To Joel Jarek DeGraff, Donna, Cosi, Gino, Tom and Dena. To the Amoruso family, Mentis family, Kouremetis family, Blair family, and the DeGraff clan.

Thank you to my editor at Putnam, Kerri Kolen, for eking out the best in me while granting me permission to create the books I love.

Thank you to Andy McNicol for having my back, always, as well as Greg Hodes, Justin Ongert, Amir Shakalilli, Strand Conover, Brooke Slavik-Jung, Ben Davis, Christian Muirhead, and my entire team at WME.

To the entire book team: Elise Loehnen, Tori Borengasser, Brett Ruttenberg, Hayley Antonian, Holly Moss, Krista Burditt, Brett Spencer, Katie Kempster, Nick Rivera, Michelle Mayer, Felisha Tolentino, Gary Mancillas, Rich Morris, Julia Wheeler, Gloria Noto, and the team at Mother New York: Piers North, Nick Feder, and Alizée Freudenthal.

To Gary Stiffelman at Greenberg Traurig for officiating at our wedding and suffering no fools and Terry Bird for managing my business.

Thank you to Charlize Theron, Kay Cannon, Laverne McKinnon, Ted Sarandos, and Netflix for immortalizing my past into something that's worth laughing at even more.

PUTNAM

G. P. Putnam's Sons
Publishers Since 1838
An imprint of Penguin Random
House LLC
375 Hudson Street
New York, New York 10014

Copyright © 2016 by Sophia
Amoruso

ISBN 9780399174889

Printed in China

Book design by Mother Design